T0323580

Cambridge Elements ≡

Elements in Health Communication
edited by
Louise Cummings
The Hong Kong Polytechnic University

PERSISTENCE OF MISINFORMATION

Biased Cognitive Processing and Polarization

Yanmengqian Zhou
University at Buffalo

Lijiang Shen
Pennsylvania State University

Shaftesbury Road, Cambridge CB2 8EA, United Kingdom

One Liberty Plaza, 20th Floor, New York, NY 10006, USA

477 Williamstown Road, Port Melbourne, VIC 3207, Australia

314–321, 3rd Floor, Plot 3, Splendor Forum, Jasola District Centre,
New Delhi – 110025, India

103 Penang Road, #05–06/07, Visioncrest Commercial, Singapore 238467

Cambridge University Press is part of Cambridge University Press & Assessment,
a department of the University of Cambridge.

We share the University's mission to contribute to society through the pursuit
of education, learning and research at the highest international levels of excellence.

www.cambridge.org
Information on this title: www.cambridge.org/9781009565349

DOI: 10.1017/9781009397339

When citing this work, please include a reference to the DOI 10.1017/9781009397339

First published 2025

A catalogue record for this publication is available from the British Library

ISBN 978-1-009-56534-9 Hardback
ISBN 978-1-009-39737-7 Paperback
ISSN 2754-1045 (online)
ISSN 2754-1037 (print)

Persistence of Misinformation

Biased Cognitive Processing and Polarization

Elements in Health Communication

DOI: 10.1017/9781009397339
First published online: January 2025

Yanmengqian Zhou
University at Buffalo

Lijiang Shen
Pennsylvania State University

Author for correspondence: Lijiang Shen, lus32@psu.edu

Abstract: Misinformation can be broadly defined as information that is inaccurate or false according to the best available evidence, or information whose validity cannot be verified. It is created and spread with or without clear intent to cause harm. There is well-documented evidence that misinformation persists despite fact-checking and the presentation of corrective information, often traveling faster and deeper than facts in the online environment. Drawing on the frameworks of social judgment theory, cognitive dissonance theory, and motivated information processing, the authors conceptualize corrective information as a generic type of counter-attitudinal message and misinformation as attitude-congruent messages. They then examine the persistence of misinformation through the lens of biased responses to attitude-inconsistent versus -consistent information. Psychological inoculation is proposed as a strategy to mitigate misinformation.

Keywords: misinformation, health communication, mitigation, inoculation strategy, psychological mechanisms

ISBNs: 9781009565349 (HB), 9781009397377 (PB), 9781009397339 (OC)
ISSNs: 2754-1045 (online), 2754-1037 (print)

Contents

1 Introduction

In 2016, Oxford Dictionaries named "post-truth" as its Word of the Year. Four years later, the term "infodemic" quickly (re)gained its popularity in 2020 as the World Health Organization (WHO) declared that we had an infodemic to fight alongside a pandemic. The explosion of misinformation and the challenge to debunk it with corrective information have played a large part in the rising prominence of these phenomena. The now infamous trilogy video *Plandemic*[1] might be the best example. The three-part (The Hidden Agenda behind COVID-19, Indoctornation, and the Great Awakening) video on COVID-19 conspiracy theory was produced by Mikki Willis and features a discredited researcher who has long been a member of the anti-vaccine community making false claims about the causes of COVID-19, various prevention measures, and vaccines. The first installment (the Hidden Agenda) quickly went viral since its release in May 2020 and became one of the most widespread COVID-19 misinformation videos, despite efforts by social media platforms to remove it from their websites. Indeed, misinformation is presented in virtually every domain, traveling faster and deeper than true information (Vosoughi et al., 2018). It was estimated that the average US adult saw and remembered 1.14 fake news stories during the 2016 presidential election period (Allcott & Gentzkow, 2017). According to a report by Stop Funding Heat (2021), there were up to 1.36 million daily views of climate misinformation on Facebook. Recently, the world has witnessed an alarmingly high rate of misinformation pertaining to the COVID-19 pandemic (Kouzy et al., 2020), to the point that United States senators wrote a letter of concern[2] to urge the social media platform Reddit to combat health misinformation. And the list goes on.

The fallout from the ubiquitous, fast-spreading misinformation is also well documented. Across various contexts, exposure to misinformation gives rise to distrust in experts and institutions, inaccurate decision-making, inaction or unproductive – sometimes fatal – actions, and an increasingly polarized, dysfunctional sociopolitical environment (Balmas, 2014; Cook, 2019; Kuklinski et al., 2000; Loomba et al., 2021). Health misinformation, in particular, has caused tremendous harm by negatively influencing individuals' health attitudes, beliefs, and behaviors, increasing societal-level mortality and morbidity burdens, and exacerbating health disparities (e.g., Pandey et al., 2023; Southwell et al., 2023; Xu et al., 2023). In response to its threat, research on misinformation has grown

---

[1] www.npr.org/2020/05/08/852451652/seen-plandemic-we-take-a-close-look-at-the-viral-conspir acy-video-s-claims

[2] https://www.lujan.senate.gov/newsroom/press-releases/lujan-klobuchar-heinrich-urge-reddit-to-combat-health-misinformation/

exponentially in recent years, tackling fundamental queries such as what it is, why it is a problem, and what to do about it, among others (Adams et al., 2023; Lewandowsky et al., 2017; Nan et al., 2023). Rooted in this literature, in this section, we first offer a definition of misinformation, followed by a review of research on the persistence of misinformation and its correction. We conclude the section by advancing two broad questions that we attempt to address in this Element: Why does misinformation persist? And what can be done to mitigate it?

Defining Misinformation

Despite the wide interest it attracts, there is currently no consensus on the definition of misinformation. A systematic review in the health context revealed that misinformation has been defined in over 30 distinct ways (Wang et al., 2022). Many of the definitions point to features such as false, inaccurate, misleading, or conflict with verifiable facts (e.g., Guess & Lyons, 2020; Krause et al., 2020; Kuklinski et al., 2000; Wardle, 2017). It is an ongoing discussion as to how these features should themselves be defined and bounded (e.g., Krause et al., 2022; Vraga & Bode, 2020). Indeed, one of the main challenges for defining misinformation is the lack of straightforward, agreed-on benchmarks that can be used to assess the truth value of information (Nan et al., 2023). To date, the two most frequently adopted standards seem to be evidence and expert opinion, although researchers rightly caution that operationalizing these standards can be difficult due to the progressive nature of knowledge and requires constant adjustment to match its current state (Nan et al., 2023; Vraga & Bode, 2020).

For our purposes, we use the dimensions of truth value and intention to harm to categorize information. First, information can be truthful and created and shared without the intention to harm (e.g., scientific facts). Second, information can be truthful and created and shared with the intention to harm (e.g., facts, evidence, and expert testimonies used to incriminate people). Third, information can be false and created and shared without the intention to harm (e.g., well-meaning but incorrect health tips). Fourth, information can be false and created and shared with the intention to harm (e.g., the Plandemic video). The last two categories are where misinformation lies. It can be broadly defined as information that is inaccurate or false, or information whose validity cannot be verified, whether or not it is created and spread with clear intent to cause harm. By this definition, disinformation, which is purposefully deceptive or misleading (Lazer et al., 2018, see also McQuade, 2024), is subsumed under misinformation. This approach allows misinformation to be identified based on message features without the need to assess motivations or intentions, which are difficult (and in some cases impossible) to discern (Treen et al., 2020). It should also be noted that multiple motivations may underlie individuals' information-seeking and sharing behaviors, such as value, control, and truth motivations (Cornwell & Higgins, 2018), as well as instrumental, hedonic, and cognitive utilities (Sharot & Sunstein, 2020, see also types of involvements, Johnson & Eagly, 1989). It is safe to assume that motivations beyond the pursuit of truth or accuracy should underlie the creation and/or spread of misinformation.

Persistence of Misinformation and Its Correction

The problem with misinformation is not only that it brings about detrimental consequences as it spreads but that it tends to be extremely resistant to correction. It persists and continues to shape beliefs, attitudes, and decision-making, even after being retracted or corrected (Ecker et al., 2014; Seifert, 2014; Thorson, 2016, see also Chan et al., 2017; Chan & Albarrcin, 2023). A frequently cited example is the MMR autism fraud. In February 1998, *The Lancet*, a high-impact medical journal, published an article led by Andrew Wakefield that fraudulently claimed a possible causal association between the MMR vaccine and autism. The UK General Medical Council later ruled that Wakefield had acted "dishonestly and irresponsibly" in his research, resulting in *The Lancet* retracting the article in February 2010. Wakefield was also struck off the UK medical register in May 2010. Despite the retraction and discredit, the vaccine-autism myth and its negative impact on vaccine uptake have persisted to this day (Fombonne et al., 2020; Novilla et al., 2023).

One might reasonably suspect that the persistence of the misinformation on the vaccine-autism link could be attributable to the twelve-year gap between the publication of Wakefield's article and its retraction. However, there is substantial evidence that misinformation endures even when correction occurs immediately after exposure (Rich & Zaragoza, 2020; Seifert, 2002), although its influence might be weakened in some cases (Chan et al., 2022; Walter & Tukachinsky, 2020). Of course, a variety of other dimensions have been carefully considered in the attempts to debunk misinformation. For example, intervention messages were designed to provide explanations of the origins of misinformation (Connor Desai & Reimers, 2023) or to be more elaborate with detailed reasoning (Ecker et al., 2019; Martel et al., 2021). Individuals were put through repeated exposure to corrective messages (Denner et al., 2023), instructed to read the corrective messages more carefully (van Oostendorp, 1996), or offered different types of literacy training (Hameleers, 2022). Different messaging strategies, such as fear appeals (Chen & Tang, 2023), narratives (Sangalang et al., 2019), and humor (Vraga et al., 2019), were employed. Researchers have also explored the potential of diverse sources (Van der Meer & Jin, 2019) and presentation formats (Pluviano et al., 2017).

To date, studies testing the effectiveness of the wide range of strategies reviewed above have produced mixed findings at best, with many failing to yield any substantial corrective effect and some leading to a backfire effect where beliefs in misinformation are strengthened rather than attenuated (Nyhan & Reifler, 2010). Indeed, a meta-analysis of twenty experiments by Chan and colleagues (2017) documented large effects for misinformation persistence, despite the observed effectiveness of debunking in discrediting misinformation. Worse yet, a detailed debunking message was found to be positively associated with the misinformation-persistent effect (Chan et al., 2017). Walter and Murphy's (2018) meta-analysis similarly revealed that, despite an overall moderate positive effect of corrective messages on reducing beliefs in misinformation, the debunking effect diminished by 60 percent when it came to real-world misinformation (as opposed to constructed misinformation). In their more recent meta-analysis, Walter and Tukachinsky (2020) observed that misinformation continues to influence beliefs even after being corrected, concluding that corrections do not eliminate misinformation. Focusing on science-relevant misinformation, Chan and Albarracín (2023) found a nonsignificant overall correction effect. In the health context, a meta-analysis including sixteen experimental studies revealed that, on average, mitigating messages were ineffective in reducing the impact of COVID-19 misinformation (Janmohamed et al., 2021). Simply put, post hoc correction or fact-checking, regardless of the strategy employed, does not have substantial utility or potency against the impact and persistence of misinformation.

Addressing the challenges of correcting, mitigating, and preventing misinformation requires a clear understanding of why misinformation resists correction and persists. It should be noted that such resistance manifests in different ways at different stages of information processing. In some cases, individuals understand, accept, and are able to recall the correction, yet their inferential reasoning still, to varying degrees, relies on misinformation (e.g., Thorson, 2016), a phenomenon that has been extensively studied within the continued influence effect paradigm. Much theorizing on this phenomenon has centered on how human memory functions (Seifert, 2002; for a review, see Ecker et al., 2022). Corrective messages, however, are also often disregarded or rejected by the recipients. Specifically, people might avoid exposing themselves and pay little attention to them, judge them as ineffective, develop counterarguments, and/or derogate the sources of the messages (e.g., Zhou & Shen, 2022). This Element focuses on the potential mechanisms underlying this process. We propose that the persistence of misinformation as a result of this resistance process can be examined as a special case of biased processing of counter-attitudinal information driven by multiple motivations, which we elaborate on in the next section.

2 The Processing of Misinformation versus Corrective Information

Misinformation may have attention-grabbing features, such as sensationalism (e.g., Staender et al., 2022) and emotional appeal (e.g., Carrasco-Farre, 2022), that make it easy to process and memorable, contributing to its dissemination and persistence (Kemp et al., 2022; Putman et al., 2017). Misinformation also frequently uses manipulation persuasive techniques, including the use of emotional language,[3] which evokes strong negative emotions; false dichotomies,[4] which present choices as if they are mutually exclusive and are the only options available; scapegoating,[5] which singles out a certain person or group and blames them for a particular issue; and ad hominem attacks,[6] which target an individual rather than their argument to redirect people's attention away from the actual problem (Roozenbeek et al., 2022). These manipulation strategies are similarly conducive to the proliferation of misinformation. However, cognitive theories suggest that the persistence of misinformation is primarily attributable to the mechanisms of information processing by individuals, rather than to the inherent features of the messages themselves.

Corrective messages aim to change individuals' existing beliefs, particularly those based on misinformation. This process involves challenging currently hold beliefs and replacing them with accurate information, making corrective messages inherently counter-attitudinal. For instance, for someone who believes that COVID-19 travels via mobile networks, a message that debunks this myth and explains how COVID-19 truly spreads inevitably refutes their prior position on the transmission of the virus. The processing of corrective information thus can be considered a special case of counter-attitudinal information processing, a phenomenon that has been extensively theorized in social psychology and communication research. We draw on social judgment theory (Sherif & Hovland 1961; Sherif et al. 1965), cognitive dissonance theory (Festinger, 1957), and motivated information processing (Chaiken et al., 1996) as three key theoretical frameworks to analyze the limited effectiveness

---

[3] https://www.youtube.com/watch?v=ER64qa_qnWg&list=PL12X50gJBPRouaAVd1RopSSJ74J5_1zVL&index=5
[4] https://www.youtube.com/watch?v=gDfQHWQwJ8Q&ab_channel=InfoInterventions
[5] https://www.youtube.com/watch?v=BdlBHh0FOtw&ab_channel=InfoInterventions
[6] https://www.youtube.com/watch?v=f6_I_KQBGXg&ab_channel=InfoInterventions

of corrective messages as counter-attitudinal information and the persistence of misinformation as attitude-congruent information. This section will first provide a brief overview of these theoretical frameworks and then present and discuss empirical evidence related to their application in understanding the enduring influence of misinformation.

Social Judgment Theory

Social judgment theory posits that the extent to which individuals are persuaded by a message depends on how they evaluate the position being advocated by the message, which further is determined by their initial beliefs (Sherif et al., 1965). In other words, attitude change is a function of the judgment of the advocacy anchored by one's prior position. For any given issue, there can be a range of possible alternative positions. For example, an individual might believe that climate change is a complete hoax or that climate change is one of the biggest challenges facing humanity. These two extremes mark the bounds of potential positions, and a person may hold a position that falls anywhere in between. Depending on where one's initial position sits, they might evaluate a position put forth by a message as within their latitude of acceptance (i.e., positions that one finds acceptable), rejection (i.e., positions that one finds unacceptable), or noncommitment (i.e., positions that one finds neither acceptable nor unacceptable).

In general, attitude-consistent information tends to reside within individuals' latitude of acceptance, whereas attitude-inconsistent information falls within their latitude of rejection (Gunther et al., 2017). The size of the latitude can vary depending on the level of ego involvement. Ego involvement refers to the extent to which an issue is of personal meaning or importance to a person (Sherif et al., 1973). Social judgment theory suggests that as the level of ego involvement increases, the latitude of rejection expands while the latitude of acceptance and noncommitment shrinks. That is, when an individual is highly involved in an issue, they will find only a small number of positions close to their existing position on the issue acceptable and reject many alternative options. Conversely, when one is less involved, they may be more open to considering a wider range of perspectives. In addition, social judgment theory posits that a message advocating for a position that falls in one's latitude of acceptance is likely to be perceived as closer to their initial position than it actually is, demonstrating an assimilation effect. In contrast, when a message advocates for a position within an individual's latitude of rejection, it is likely to be perceived as more distant from their position than it actually is, an effect known as the contrast effect (Sherif et al., 1965).

Attitude change, according to social judgment theory, depends on where the position advocated in a message is perceived to be located. A message that advocates a position judged to be in the latitude of acceptance or noncommitment is likely to bring about attitude change in the intended direction. A message that advocates a position perceived to be in the latitude of rejection, on the other hand, is unlikely to yield attitude change in the desired direction and in some cases might even cause backfire, producing attitude change in the opposite direction. As such, the greatest amount of attitude change is expected to occur in cases where the message is the most discrepant from an individual's existing position but does not yet reach their latitude of rejection.

Social judgment theory has clear implications for understanding the persistence of misinformation. When misinformation on a given issue is adopted, it establishes an anchor against which any subsequent issue-relevant messages, including corrective information, are judged. It should be clarified here that susceptibility to misinformation (i.e., the initial adoption of misinformation) is beyond the scope of this Element. Interested readers may refer to works such as van Der Linden (2022) and Nan et al. (2022) for a systematic review. Insofar as corrective information presents positions that are in direct contrast to one's initial position rooted in misinformation, it likely resides in their latitude of rejection. This is especially true for individuals who are highly involved in the issue in question and hence have a relatively narrow latitude of acceptance. Indeed, misinformation tends to be most prevalent and impactful in highly divisive areas that touch on fundamental personal values, such as COVID-19 vaccines, political elections, and climate change. Accordingly, as the theory predicts, corrective information is often unable to produce attitude change and, worse yet, may potentially strengthen existing belief in misinformation.

Cognitive Dissonance Theory

Theories centered on cognitive consistency provide another useful lens for understanding the ineffectiveness of corrections. Cognitive dissonance theory (Festinger, 1957) is a prominent example of this group of theories (see also balance theory, Heider, 1946; congruity theory, Osgood & Tannenbaum, 1955). The theory starts with the idea that people have cognitions that share different types of relations. They can be *irrelevant* to one another. For example, a positive attitude toward vaccination likely has nothing to do with whether or not one likes cats. When two cognitions are relevant, they can further be *consonant* or *dissonant* with each other. Consonant cognitions are consistent such that one follows from the other. The belief that human-caused climate change is a serious threat and a favorable attitude toward sustainable products are two consonant cognitive elements. Cognitions are dissonant when the opposite of one follows from the other. A negative attitude toward mammograms and the belief that mammograms can reduce the risk of dying from breast cancer are dissonant in that what follows the risk-reduction cognition should be a positive attitude toward mammograms. The theory posits that a person experiences dissonance – a psychologically uncomfortable state that motivates its reduction – when two cognitions are dissonant.

The magnitude of dissonance varies depending on the ratio of dissonant to consonant cognitions and the importance of cognitions. A suggested formula for the dissonance ratio is to divide the number of dissonant cognitions by the total number of dissonant and consonant cognitions (Beauvois & Joule, 1996; Harmon-Jones & Mills, 2019). Each cognition is further weighted by its importance. As the number or importance of dissonance elements increases and the number or importance of consonance elements decreases, the magnitude of dissonance experienced increases. The greater the magnitude of dissonance, the greater the pressure or motivation one has to reduce it. As suggested by the factors influencing the magnitude of dissonance, there are a variety of ways through which one may reduce dissonance, including adding new consonant cognitions, removing or changing dissonant cognitions, increasing the importance of consonant cognitions, and decreasing the importance of dissonant cognitions.

Considered one of the most influential social psychological theories, cognitive dissonance theory has been applied to study a variety of phenomena. One prominent line of this research focuses on how individuals respond to counter-attitudinal messages. Information that is inconsistent with existing cognition would presumably arouse dissonance. Since dissonance is an uncomfortable state that people are driven to avoid or reduce, they are likely to seek out and attend to information that is consistent with their current cognitions while avoiding cognition-incongruent messages. Substantial empirical evidence has been documented in support of this general prediction (e.g., Garrett & Stroud, 2014; Knobloch-Westerwick & Meng, 2011). When avoidance is not an option, counter-attitudinal messages tend to be denied or misinterpreted to be consistent with one's prior cognition to reduce dissonance (Harmon-Jones & Mills, 2019). Specific to the case of misinformation, belief in misinformation can be seen as a current cognitive element, and messages presented to correct the misconception are, therefore, dissonant with the current cognition. Cognitive dissonance theory thus suggests that misinformation-believing individuals are motivated to dismiss the dissonance-arousing corrective messages and may even misinterpret these messages in a distorted way that further strengthens their current beliefs, as reflected in the frequently observed boomerang effect (e.g., Zhao & Fink, 2021).

The selectivity in exposure, attention, and information utilization in decision-making mentioned above (see also Ahluwalia, 2000) can lead to another phenomenon contributing to the persistence of misinformation, especially when exposure to misinformation precedes exposure to the facts. That phenomenon is illusory correlation. Illusory correlation occurs when individuals infer or believe there is a relationship between two factors or events when there is actually none; for example, the perceived link between the MMR vaccines and autism and the misperception that influenza vaccines give people the flu. Pre-existing biases, stereotypes, and perspectives might further exacerbate the fallacy of illusory correlation. In a Twitter (now known as X) post, then-president Donald Trump claimed[7] that we need global warming, citing the extreme cold weather in the Midwest as evidence. The label "global warming" might lead people to interpret colder weather as evidence that climate change is a hoax out of the liberal agenda, which actually constitutes evidence that climate change is real and worsening (i.e., more extreme weather).

Motivated Information Processing

Whether driven by the discomfort of cognitive dissonance or by being situated within the latitude of rejection, the previous two frameworks provide insights into a more automatic motivational process underlying the failure to accept corrections. In these instances, individuals' goals are often implicit and largely unconscious. However, motivation can also be more deliberate, with goals that are explicit and actively pursued. This third framework emphasizes this more intentional aspect. Accuracy motivation, the desire to arrive at valid attitudes and beliefs that correspond with objective reality, is believed to be the most functional goal underlying information processing (Chaiken et al., 1996). When accuracy-motivated, individuals tend to use cognitive strategies that are most appropriate, engage in deeper and more careful processing of information, and subsequently reach more accurate conclusions (Kunda, 1990). For example, an individual who wants to develop a valid understanding of COVID-19 vaccines is primarily driven by accuracy. Since their goal is to be accurate, as they are exposed to different types of information, they are likely to engage in unbiased and thorough processing with an open mind. Of course, people do not always process information with accuracy motivation. They might also be driven by defense goals. Defense motivation is the desire

---

[7] https://people.com/politics/donald-trump-need-global-warming-extreme-cold-midwest/

to hold attitudes and beliefs that are congruent with one's self-definition (Chaiken et al., 1996). When defense-motivated, individuals seek to preserve their self-concept, leading to biased information processing that yields conclusions consistent with their values, identities, interests, or attributes. Similar to defense motivation, impression motivation – the desire to express attitudes and beliefs that satisfy interpersonal and social goals in a given context – also leads to biased information processing (Chaiken et al., 1996). Specifically, individuals who are impression-motivated tend to use selective processing strategies that result in conclusions conducive to social acceptance. While more than one motivation may coexist in any given setting, meaning individuals may not be *solely* driven by one of these motivations, in most cases they are *primarily* accuracy-, defense-, or impression-motivated (Chen & Chaiken, 1999).

In the context of misinformation correction, defense motivation likely prevails over other motivations. Consider for a moment the most widely spread and impactful misinformation in real-world settings. It is mostly about politics (e.g., "Barack Obama was not born in America"), health (e.g., "COVID-19 vaccines contain location-tracking microchips"), science (e.g., "climate change is a hoax"), and other topics that tend to have clear implications for personal values, identities, and worldviews (Walter & Murphy, 2018). As people attend to, retain, and develop false perceptions based on misinformation on these issues, it likely becomes a part of their self-defining beliefs and attitudes. When corrective information is presented to change these beliefs and attitudes, it would then conceivably activate the fundamental motivation to protect the integrity of the self (Sherman & Cohen, 2002), perhaps more so than it activates the motivation to achieve accuracy or obtain social acceptance given its close tie to the core self-concept (Chaiken et al., 1996). When defense motivation dominates, as the theory suggests, people engage in biased processing where attitude-incongruent information (i.e., corrective information) receives negative responses, be it inattentiveness, biased assimilation, and/or counterarguing, to reinforce their pre-existing attitudes (e.g., Hart & Nisbet, 2012; Wischnewski & Krämer, 2020), resulting in attitude polarization and more entrenched positions, hence, the persistence of misinformation. Although there is evidence that politically conservative people are more prone to such biases (e.g., Enders et al., 2023), it occurs in liberal individuals as well. A good example is the recent Sokal Hoax Squared.[8] Three scholars wrote twenty fake articles using popular jargons and submitted them to high-impact, peer-reviewed journals. Seven of those articles were

---

[8] https://www.theatlantic.com/ideas/archive/2018/10/new-sokal-hoax/572212/

accepted for publication. As this example shows, editors and reviewers of academic journals can easily fall prey to this fallacy, regardless of their knowledge and intelligence.[9]

Distinct motivations are further associated with distinct modes of processing. Within the framework of the heuristic-systematic model (HSM, Chaiken et al., 1989, see also Kahneman, 2013), high accuracy motivation is thought to promote systematic processing, which involves effortful and analytical thinking, particularly when the capacity to engage in such processing is also present. In contrast, strong defense motivation is likely to give rise to heuristic processing, a relatively effortless mode in which simple decision rules are applied, especially when individuals' cognitive ability is limited and/or when the message contains congenial cues (Chaiken et al., 1996). Similarly, the elaboration likelihood model (ELM, Petty & Cacioppo, 1986) theorizes the distinction between the central and peripheral routes of processing, with the former characterized by careful evaluation and scrutiny of the information and the latter by the use of simple cues to make judgments. The ELM also argues that the mode of information processing is determined by motivation and ability. When an individual's attitudes toward an issue are primarily concerned with their goals and desired outcomes, they have high outcome-relevant involvement (Johnson & Eagly, 1989) and tend to follow the central route of processing when they have to ability to do so. When an attitude is linked primarily with one's values, which Johnson & Eagly (1989) termed value-relevant involvement, the peripheral route of processing is more likely to be followed, often in a biased manner. To the extent that accuracy motivation – the dominance of which underpins the logic of corrective strategies – is likely preceded by nonaccuracy motivations, it follows that the effectiveness of corrections is limited. In such cases, individuals are likely to engage in superficial processing where consistency cues exert a greater influence on message acceptance or denial.

Evidence from Two Empirical Studies

Guided by the overarching question of why/how misinformation persists, we collected two datasets on the topics of vaccines and climate change, respectively (Shen & Zhou, 2021; Zhou & Shen, 2022). Here, we review the findings from both studies and discuss their implications for understanding the persistence of misinformation through the frameworks of social judgment theory, cognitive dissonance theory, and motivated information processing.

---

[9] https://www.bbc.com/future/article/20200406-why-smart-people-believe-coronavirus-myths

Main Hypotheses and Study Design

Both studies offer an empirical test of our hypothesis that the persistence of misinformation may stem from biased processing of corrective messages, a type of counter-attitudinal information. Specifically, across the two studies, we sought to investigate (a) how patterns and outcomes of processing misinformation and corrective information vary depending on recipients' pre-existing positions, and (b) the mechanisms that underlie the persistence of misinformation and attitude polarization. We predicted that both individuals with accurate and misinformation-informed prior beliefs would demonstrate biased processing favoring their existing attitudes, with the effect being more pronounced and impactful among those holding inaccurate beliefs when exposed to corrective messages.

Both studies employed a web-based experimental design with pre-existing positions and message type as between-subjects factors. In the vaccine study, vaccine-inclined ($n = 658$) and -hesitant individuals ($n = 338$) were randomly assigned to watch either a video presenting scientific evidence refuting the vaccine-autism link or a misinformation video supporting the link. Similarly, in the climate change study, climate change believers ($n = 208$) and deniers ($n = 200$) were randomly assigned to watch pro-climate change (scientific) or anti-climate change (misinformation) messages. To introduce message heterogeneity and improve generalizability, this study employed a multiple-message design where participants watched three randomly ordered messages. Participants for both studies were recruited through Qualtrics, watched the assigned video(s), and responded to questions on information processing and perceptions, outcomes, individual differences, and demographics. Full details on the design, procedure, and measures can be found in Shen and Zhou (2021) and Zhou and Shen (2022).

Processing Corrective Messages as Counter-Attitudinal Information

Across both studies, we found strong evidence of biased responses to messages as a function of pre-existing attitudes. Specifically, pre-existing attitude interacted with message type (i.e., scientific/corrective versus misinformation) in predicting source and message perceptions and empathy (see Table 1 in Zhou & Shen [2022] for estimated marginal means). Climate change believers judged the source of scientific evidence as more trustworthy and expert than the source of misinformation, and perceived scientific information as more factual, effective, and eliciting greater empathy than misinformation. The exact opposite pattern was observed with climate change deniers: they rated scientific information lower on all these dimensions compared to misinformation. In the vaccine study, both vaccine-inclined and -hesitant individuals judged the source of misinformation as less trustworthy and expert than the source of scientific/ corrective message, but the difference was statistically significant only among vaccine-inclined people (see Figure 3 in Shen & Zhou [2021]). For vaccine-hesitant individuals, no significant difference was found in source evaluations between scientific and misinformation messages. Similarly, vaccine-inclined individuals perceived scientific information as significantly more effective and factual than misinformation, while vaccine-hesitant individuals showed no significant difference in these perceptions (see Figure 1 in Shen & Zhou [2021]). Findings from both studies clearly support the biased responses to corrections as counter-attitudinal information among misinformation believers, as theorized in social judgment theory, cognitive dissonance theory, and the motivated information processing framework.

The results from the vaccine study warrant some elaboration, as the observed patterns were not as straightforward as those in the climate change study. Specifically, the lack of difference in source and message evaluations among vaccine-hesitant individuals suggests the influence of heuristic processing, driven by defense motivation. Chaiken et al. (1996) termed this mechanism as defensive inattention where counter-attitudinal messages are ignored or super-ficially processed, allowing quick judgments based on general congruency heuristics that reinforce prior beliefs. An alternative mechanism in which bias or selectivity can manifest is the generation of counterarguments, which requires more systematic scrutiny of counter-attitudinal information to identify its flaws (Chaiken et al., 1996). The clear distinction in source and message evaluations among vaccine-inclined individuals can be inferred as evidence for systematic processing. The use of different types of processing (i.e., heuristic versus systematic) among vaccine-hesitant and -inclined individuals further speaks to the distinct motivations that might be driving people who believe in misinformation and those who hold a correct existing position as well as their varying levels of processing ability when encountering counter-attitudinal information. Vaccine-hesitant individuals, for example, appear driven primarily by defense motivation, coupled with limited processing ability when faced with pro-vaccine messages. Indeed, research shows that vaccine-hesitant individuals are more concerned with the moral implications of vaccines – such as issues of purity and personal liberties, which are closely tied to self-identity that underlie defense motivation – than with the objective health benefits that would align with accuracy motivation (Amin et al., 2017; Reich, 2016). In line with these findings, in our study, vaccine-hesitant individuals reported a significantly higher level of value-relevant involvement, a construct similar to defense motivation, than vaccine-inclined individuals. From a cognitive ability perspective, vaccine-hesitant individuals may be constrained by epistemic egocentrism, which is the inability to take any perspectives that are not their own (Motta et al., 2018; Nagel, 2010). Of course, the same cognitive constraint is likely also experienced by vaccine-inclined individuals in the face of anti-vaccine messages. However, for this group, their ability to process scientific information remains intact. In addition, their primary concerns, largely focused on harm reduction and fairness (Amin et al., 2017), suggest that accuracy motivation likely outweighs defense motivation in their case. It should be clarified that accuracy and defense motivations may co-exist for both vaccine-inclined and -hesitant individuals. However, unlike for the former where these motivations are compatible, they are in conflict with each other for the latter where defense motivation likely takes priority over accuracy motivation, resulting in a superficial processing of corrective information. In summary, consistent with our conceptualizing of corrective messages as a type of counter-attitudinal information, the results suggest that vaccine misinformation believers tend to engage in heuristic processing of pro-vaccine messages, driven by defense motivation. This leads to the ineffectiveness of corrective messages and the persistence of their misbelief.

The different ways in which people with misinformation-informed positions and those holding correct positions respond to counter-attitudinal messages were also evident in the climate change study. Although as reviewed previously, both groups responded more negatively to counter-attitudinal videos and more positively to attitude-consistent videos, the biased response pattern was more extreme among climate change deniers (i.e., misinformation believers). A stronger biased pattern means that at least one of the following three configurations should occur: (1) climate change deniers exposed to scientific information score lower on perceived source expertise and trustworthiness, empathy, and perceived message factuality and effectiveness than climate change believers exposed to misinformation (i.e., greater extremity in response to attitude-inconsistent messages); (2) climate change deniers exposed to misinformation score higher on the aforementioned variables than believers exposed to scientific information (i.e., greater extremity in response to attitude-consistent messages); (3) the difference between ratings of misinformation and scientific information is greater among deniers than believers (i.e., greater relative extremity in message responses). As shown in Table 2 of Zhou and Shen (2022), the difference between evaluations of and empathy toward misinformation and scientific information was consistently larger among climate change deniers than believers. In addition, compared to believers, deniers demonstrated greater extremity in their responses to (1) attitude-inconsistent messages (i.e., corrective information), with lower ratings across all variables, and (2) attitude-consistent messages (i.e., misinformation), with higher ratings across all variables, except perceived factuality.

The implications of this set of findings align closely with those from the vaccine study, suggesting that individuals who believe in misinformation are primarily driven by defense motivation. They engage in biased processing of corrective information in ways that reinforce rather than challenge their existing beliefs. This implied strong defense motivation among this group is unsurprising given that, like vaccines, misbeliefs about climate change are often deeply rooted in values, worldviews, and sociopolitical identities (Newman et al., 2018; Zia & Todd, 2010). The increasingly moralized discourse surrounding these issues likely amplifies defense motivation, as it threatens their core beliefs (Giner-Sorolila & Chaiken, 1997; Täuber et al., 2015). From the perspective of social judgment theory, the findings also suggest that these individuals likely have a large latitude of rejection, perhaps due to high ego involvement, making it particularly challenging to change their attitude.

Moderators of Biased Processing of Counter-Attitudinal Messages

Three moderators of biased processing were tested across the two studies, including value-relevant involvement, outcome-relevant involvement, and attitude certainty. Examining these moderators enhances our understanding of when biased responses are more likely to occur and how pronounced they are. These individual difference variables also provide insights into which individuals are more resistant to corrections, which is crucial for understanding societal attitude polarization.

To review, value-relevant involvement refers to "the psychological state that is created by the activation of attitudes that are linked to important values" (Johnson & Eagly, 1989, p. 290), whereas outcome-relevant involvement arises when one's attitudes are primarily concerned with their currently important goals and outcomes (Johnson & Eagly, 1989). Johnson and Eagly (1989) theorized that value-relevant involvement aligns conceptually with ego involvement within the framework of social judgment theory (Sherif et al., 1965). It is also considered similar to Chaiken et al.'s (1996) discussion of defense motivation. The construct of outcome-relevant involvement, on the other hand, was developed to provide a more precise representation of what Petty and Cacioppo (1979) termed issue involvement, which is conceptually related to accuracy motivation as theorized by Chaiken et al. (1996).

As discussed earlier, vaccine-hesitant and -inclined individuals tend to have concerns over different aspects of vaccines (e.g., Amin et al., 2017). Therefore, we anticipated that the types of involvement would have different impacts on their message processing. Specifically, we expected that value-relevant involvement would intensify biased processing among the vaccine-hesitant but not the vaccine-inclined. This implies that (1) there would be an interaction between value-relevant involvement and message type in predicting message perceptions among the vaccine-hesitant, where those with high value-relevant involvement would show no difference in message assessment, while those with low value-relevant involvement would exhibit differential judgments of misinformation and scientific information; and (2) value-relevant involvement would not interact with message type in predicting message perceptions among vaccine-inclined individuals. In a similar vein, we predicted that outcome-relevant involvement would amplify message processing among the vaccine-inclined but not the vaccine-hesitant. This means that (1) there would be an interaction between outcome-relevant involvement and message type in predicting message perceptions among the vaccine-inclined, where those with high outcome-relevant involvement would demonstrate greater differences in their evaluations of scientific information and misinformation than those with low outcome-relevant involvement; and (2) outcome-relevant involvement would not interact with message type in predicting message perceptions among the vaccine-hesitant.

Our results showed that there was no significant interaction between value-relevant involvement and message type in predicting message perceptions among the vaccine-inclined; this interaction was also nonsignificant among the vaccine-hesitant. However, we observed a significant interaction between outcome-relevant involvement and message type in predicting vaccine-inclined individuals' perceived message factuality. Surprisingly, the difference in perceived factuality across scientific information and misinformation appeared to be more pronounced among the vaccine-inclined who had lower levels of outcome-relevant involvement. Also unexpected was the finding that the interaction was significant among the vaccine-hesitant as well. Those with a high level of outcome-relevant involvement rated misinformation as more factual than scientific information, whereas those with a low level of outcome-relevant involvement judged scientific information as more factual than misinformation. This set of findings concerning outcome-relevant involvement seems to suggest that (1) for those holding a correct position, greater relevance of personal goals and outcomes may inhibit polarized assessments of both messages that are consistent with and contradict their existing position, reflecting a more open-minded treatment of information (Chaiken, 1987); and (2) for misinformation believers, higher levels of outcome-involvement may reinforce selectivity, which is perhaps linked to the particular outcomes they are likely concerned with (e.g., the harm of vaccines impurity). Overall, our findings did not offer clear support for the moderating effects of value- or outcome-relevant involvement. We speculate that rather than the general type of involvement, it may be the specific content within these types of involvement (e.g., fairness versus liberty in value-relevant outcomes or concerns about disease harm versus vaccine impurity in outcome-relevant outcomes) that shapes information processing. This speculation, of course, requires further empirical testing.

Focused on attitude properties, in the climate change study, we tested the moderating effect of attitude certainty. Attitude functions to facilitate the organization and sense-making of stimuli. Attitude certainty, a metacognitive attribute of attitude that pertains to the sense of conviction with which individuals hold their attitude, plays a crucial role in the performance of its function (Petrocelli et al., 2007). More certain attitudes tend to be more accessible and are automatically activated when one encounters the relevant attitude object (Fazio, 2007). As such, when confronted with counter-attitudinal information, people with higher levels of attitude certainty are likely to exhibit a stronger pattern of biased processing (Brannon et al., 2007; van Strien et al., 2016). That is, misinformation believers who firmly deny human-caused climate change are likely to evaluate the source and message of misinformation more favorably and those of scientific/corrective information more unfavorably than individuals who are less certain in their erroneous beliefs. Conversely, for individuals with a correct pre-existing position, we expect to observe the opposite pattern. Those who are highly certain of their beliefs should report more positive perceptions of scientific/ corrective information and more negative perceptions of misinformation than those with a low level of attitude certainty. This means that (1) there should be a three-way interaction among pre-existing position, message type, and attitude certainty, (2) the marginal means of the interaction between pre-existing position and message type should be consistent with the biased processing pattern, and (3) the effect size of the interaction between pre-existing position and message type should be larger at high levels of attitude certainty compared to low levels.

In line with our predictions, we observed a significant three-way interaction among pre-existing position, message type, and attitude certainty in predicting perceived source trustworthiness and expertise, empathy, and perceived message effectiveness and factuality. The marginal means of the interaction between pre-existing position and message type consistently demonstrated a polarized pattern across all models, with attitude-consistent messages being perceived more positively and counter-attitudinal ones more negatively. This polarization appeared to be stronger at higher levels of attitude certainty. The intensifying effect of attitude certainty has obvious implications for understanding the persistence of misinformation as well as for misinformation mitigation strategies. To the extent that the frequency and recency of attitude activation and retrieval tend to enhance accessibility and application (Higgins, 1996), the intense presentation of corrective information may inadvertently reinforce belief in misinformation. Not only is this approach ineffective in changing misconceptions, but it may also heighten individuals' conviction in their erroneous beliefs by making those beliefs more accessible, thereby contributing to a stronger pattern of biased processing. As a result, misinformation could become more persistent and resistant to change in the long run (Chan et al., 2017). Practically, then, we are faced with a dilemma. On the one hand, it is not an option to not intervene; on the other hand, frequent and intense corrections might make the erroneous beliefs more salient and, through biased processing, eventually more ingrained. The timing of the correction thus emerges as a critical consideration, which we will explore in greater detail in Section 3.

Consequences of Biased Processing: Misinformation Persistence, Polarization, and More

To understand the mechanisms underlying the persistence of misinformation, we proposed and tested a model informed by cognitive response theories, conceptualizing misinformation persistence as a result of cognitive responses to both the message and its source. Specifically, we examined how pre-existing position and message type interact to shape perceptions and responses toward the source and message, which, in turn, predict persuasion outcomes. To facilitate the interpretation of path coefficients, instead of directly testing the pre-existing position by message type interaction, we tested the model within each message type. That is, we estimated two separate models: one based on data from the group exposed to misinformation and the other from the group exposed to scientific information. In both models, pre-existing position served as the exogenous variable. The interaction effect, although not directly observed in the models, can be inferred from the differences in corresponding parameters across the two models. Pre-existing position had direct paths to all endogenous variables. Perceived source expertise and trustworthiness, perceived message factuality, and empathy were allowed to covary and were specified to predict perceived message effectiveness, which further had a direct path to post-exposure attitudes on climate change. Furthermore, post-exposure attitude was expected to predict post-exposure policy preferences. In addition, considering prior evidence that empathy can elicit automatic reactions (Preston & de

Waal, 2002; Shen, 2010), empathy was specified to have a direct impact on post-exposure policy preferences.

Both models had a reasonable fit to the data, and the final obtained models with the standardized path coefficients are presented in Figure 2 in Zhou and Shen (2022). In the misinformation model, pre-existing position was significantly associated with all exogenous variables, with the exception of perceived message effectiveness. Compared to climate change believers, climate change deniers judged the source of misinformation as more trustworthy and knowledgeable, assessed its content as more factual, and experienced greater empathy toward misinformation. They also had a less accurate attitude toward climate change and a lower intention to support pro-climate policies, such as market incentives to reduce industry emissions. Their source perceptions and empathy were positively linked to perceived message effectiveness. Those who experienced more empathy toward misinformation reported a less accurate post-exposure attitude, which was positively associated with support for pro-climate policies. Lastly, not surprisingly, those who perceived misinformation messages as more effective also reported a lower intention to support pro-climate policies.

Data from participants exposed to scientific/corrective information showed that pre-existing position had a significant association with all endogenous variables. Compared to individuals holding a correct position, misinformation believers rated the source of scientific information as less expert and trustworthy, perceived the message as less factual, and had less empathy toward scientific information. This group also evaluated scientific information as less effective, reported a less accurate attitude toward climate change, and was less likely to support pro-climate policies. Source perceptions, empathy, and perceived factuality were positively associated with perceived message effectiveness, which further had a positive relationship with post-exposure attitudes and support for pro-climate policy. Moreover, perceived source expertise and factuality positively predicted post-exposure attitudes, which subsequently had a positive impact on support for pro-climate policies. Overall, the findings support our hypothesized model of misinformation persistence, showing that biased responses to attitude-congruent and -incongruent information act as cognitive mediators that ultimately lead to a more polarized attitude and policy preference where prior opinions are sustained and reinforced rather than changed.

Interestingly, a comparison of the two models, particularly regarding the predictors of post-exposure attitudes, indicates that scientific information and misinformation might be processed in distinct ways. In the model of scientific information, post-exposure attitudes were directly predicted by perceived message effectiveness. In this case, empathy did not have a direct impact on attitude. In the model of misinformation, in contrast, empathy directly predicted attitude while perceived effectiveness did not have a direct association with it. Insofar as perceived message effectiveness can be considered an overall cognitive evaluation of messages (Dillard et al., 2007) whereas empathy operates as a more automatic process (Shen, 2010), these findings imply that scientific information tends to engage individuals through a more effortful cognitive process while misinformation appears to influence through a more automatic response. Considering that systematic processing requires both motivation and ability, this observation further highlights the challenges of effectively correcting misconceptions with scientific information as well as explains the prevalence and persistence of misinformation.

We also considered the impact of biased processing on information-seeking and public deliberation intentions. Considering their potential to create and reinforce information echo chambers (Knobloch-Westerwick et al., 2015), these outcomes have clear implications for our understanding of misinformation persistence and attitude polarization over time. Given the different motivations that likely underlie the information processing of individuals holding a correct position versus those holding an incorrect one, we anticipated that the intention to seek further information and engage in conversations with others who disagree on the topic would be differentially shaped by message and source perceptions for the two groups. Data from the vaccine study showed that among vaccine-inclined individuals, the intention to seek further information was positively associated with perceived source expertise and perceived factuality, but not with perceived source trustworthiness or perceived message effectiveness. In addition, both value- and outcome-relevant involvement also positively predicted information-seeking intention among this group, with z-tests indicating that outcome-relevant involvement had a significantly larger effect than value-relevant involvement. Information-seeking intentions of the vaccine-hesitant individuals, on the other hand, were positively predicted by perceived factuality and message effectiveness, but not by source perceptions. Both types of involvement were also positively associated with information-seeking intentions among vaccine-hesitant individuals, but the effects were similar in size with no significant difference. With regard to public deliberation intention, among the vaccine-inclined, it was positively predicted by perceived source expertise and perceived factuality and negatively predicted by perceived message effectiveness. Perceived source trustworthiness did not have a significant impact on deliberation intention. Moreover, deliberation intention among this group was negatively associated with value-relevant involvement and positively associated with outcome-relevant involvement. For the vaccine-hesitant, none of the message or source perception variables predicted their deliberation intention. Their deliberation intention was similarly negatively predicted by value-relevant involvement and positively predicted by outcome-relevant involvement, but to a lesser degree compared to their vaccine-inclined counterparts.

Overall, the results were consistent with our prediction that vaccine-hesitant and -inclined individuals' information-seeking and deliberation intentions were driven differentially by source and message perceptions. These perceptions, as a function of biased processing tied to pre-existing attitudes, may ultimately contribute to increased polarization and extremism in the public discourse. Notably, the observation that outcome-relevant involvement overall motivated vaccine-inclined individuals more than their vaccine-hesitant counterparts and that source and message perceptions were more reliable at predicting the intentions of vaccine-inclined than -hesitant individuals (especially with regard to the intention to engage in public deliberation) indicates that those who believe in misinformation are less driven by accuracy motivations and cognitive processes. Instead, they are motivated more by unreasoned rather than reasoned influences (Fishbein & Ajzen, 2010). This pattern mirrors our findings from the climate change study, highlighting an important perspective on the limited effectiveness of corrective information presenting scientific facts and the enduring nature of misinformation.

Summary

Conceptualizing misinformation as attitude-congruent information and corrective information as counter-attitudinal, we drew on multiple theoretical frameworks from social psychology and communication research to discuss the persistence of misinformation as a function of biased processing guided by pre-existing attitudes. From the perspective of social judgment theory, misinformation as attitude-consistent messages resides within individuals' latitude of acceptance, whereas corrective information as attitude-inconsistent messages falls within their latitude of rejection. Individuals who hold a misinformed position often perceive the issues at stake as personally significant, which expands their latitude of rejection that renders corrective messages ineffective. Within the framework of cognitive dissonance theory, when faced with information that is inconsistent with their pre-existing attitudes, the resulting psychological discomfort motivates individuals to reduce their cognitive dissonance, often by dismissing or denying the conflicting information. Along this reasoning, when misinformation believers encounter corrective information that presents claims and arguments that contradict their beliefs, they are inclined to reject it to alleviate cognitive dissonance. The framework of motivated information processing suggests that biased processing occurs when people prioritize motivations other than accuracy. Substantial evidence suggests that people who believe in misinformation tend to have a strong defense motivation that overrides their accuracy motivation. They thus have a tendency to selectively process information in ways that reinforce their pre-existing attitudes that are congruent with their self-identity.

These theoretical frameworks all provide valuable insights into the persistence of misinformation as biased processing of attitude-consistent versus -inconsistent information. Evidence from two studies in the contexts of climate change and vaccines provided strong empirical support, showing that message type and pre-existing position interactively shaped source and message perceptions and processing such that individuals with erroneous beliefs preferred misinformation and evaluated scientific/corrective information negatively. Although a similar biased pattern was observed among those with correct pre-existing positions, it was much less strong and extreme. In addition, pragmatically speaking, biased processing is not counter-productive for this group, unlike for those holding misinformed beliefs. The cognitive mechanisms identified further help explain the persistence of misinformation and the polarization of opinions on important public issues.

3 Inoculation as a Mitigation Strategy

Having established that corrective messages presented after misinformation is retained have limited effectiveness due to biased processing guided by pre-existing beliefs (i.e., beliefs in misinformation), we now shift our focus in this section to potential strategies for mitigating misinformation. We propose that psychological inoculation can be a particularly useful tool for combating misinformation. In the following sections, we will first review the literature on psychological inoculation and then discuss its utility for inducing resistance to and curtailing misinformation in the long term. Supporting empirical evidence will be integrated throughout our discussion.

Psychological Inoculation Theory

The origins of the inoculation theory can be traced back to a study by Lumsdaine and Janis (1953), which examined the effectiveness of one- versus two-sided messages in producing resistance to subsequent counterarguments. They found that while presenting only supportive arguments (i.e., one-sided message) and both supportive and opposing arguments (i.e., two-sided message) were equally effective in changing attitudes, two-sided messages were superior in sustaining attitude change when faced with subsequent counter-persuasion. This finding led the authors to conclude that recipients of two-sided messages were "given an advanced basis for ignoring or discounting the opposing communication and, thus 'inoculated'" (Lumsdaine & Janis, 1953, p. 318).

Building on this foundation and with a series of experiments (e.g., McGuire, 1961, 1962; McGuire & Papageorgis, 1962; Papageorgis & McGuire, 1961), McGuire (1964) theorized an inoculation approach to producing resistance against persuasion. The term "inoculation" stemmed from a biological analogy. The basic idea is that just as individuals can be immunized against a virus, their attitudes and beliefs can also be protected from persuasive attack through inoculation. In a medical context, individuals receive a weakened dose of the virus to build defenses or antibodies against attacks from that virus when they are exposed to it in the future. The weakened dose is supposed to help establish resistance but is not too strong to cause any illnesses itself. Applying this concept to persuasion, McGuire (1964) proposed that an inoculation message that warns people of a potential future attack on their attitude by presenting a weakened counter-attitudinal argument that can activate defense responses but is not too strong to persuade confers resistance to counter-influence.

To be consistent with the biological analogy, McGuire and colleagues' early research limited the beliefs used in their experiments to cultural truisms, which McGuire (1964) defined as "beliefs that are so widely shared within the person's social milieu that he [sic] would not have heard them attacked, and indeed, would doubt that an attack was possible" (p. 201). These could be, for example, beliefs in the benefits of tooth brushing or the utility of penicillin. However, as the theory has been applied to a wider range of topics, including controversial issues such as genetically modified foods or the legalization of marijuana, the concept of cultural truism is no longer a relevant boundary condition for inoculation research (Banas & Rains, 2010; Compton & Pfau, 2005).

In testing the resistance effect, inoculation research more or less follows a standardized set of procedures, which typically starts with a pretreatment. This pretreatment may involve a one-sided message presenting only supportive arguments, in which case it is considered a supportive pretreatment. More commonly, however, the pretreatment consists of a two-sided message that presents arguments that challenge one's current beliefs or attitudes, followed by refutations, making it a refutational pretreatment. Refutations can either be integrated into the message itself (i.e., passive refutation) or generated by individuals as part of the experimental protocol (i.e., active refutation). In a prototypical inoculation study, all participants are exposed to an attack message, but only some receive a pretreatment, which can either be supportive or refutational. This design allows researchers to evaluate the effectiveness of the attack message and determine whether (and which type of) pretreatment is effective in building resistance against the attack. In one of their classic experiments, for example, McGuire and Papageorgis (1961) observed that participants who received only the attack message scored an average of 6.64 on beliefs related to cultural altruism on a scale ranging from 1 to 15, suggesting that the attack was effective. They subsequently compared the post-counterargument beliefs of participants who received either a supportive or a refutational pretreatment and found that those who received the refutational pretreatment, regardless of its format, consistently retained a stronger belief after the attack message than those who received the supportive pretreatment. This, along with findings from many subsequent inoculation studies, provided clear evidence that refutational pretreatment is more effective in conferring resistance. In his theorizing, McGuire provided a comprehensive account of why and how refutational pretreatment works, emphasizing two key constructs: threat and refutational preemption. In addition, the role of time (i.e., the delay between treatment and attack) also appears to be a critical factor in understanding the effectiveness of inoculation.

Threat

Since its early development, inoculation theory has emphasized the central role of threat, positing that its effectiveness relies on the presentation of a threatening warning about impending arguments against one's attitudes (McGuire, 1964). That is, to successfully create resistance, it is essential to induce a sense of threat such that individuals are motivated to defend their current beliefs. As Compton (2013) highlighted, threat within the inoculation framework is not an inherent quality of the message; rather, it arises as a response to it. Thus, the key lies in individuals' perceived threat, which is believed to prompt the recognition of the vulnerability of their beliefs. This realization of vulnerability further motivates them invest effort in building defenses to protect their attitudes.

Individuals may develop threat perceptions simply from encountering arguments that oppose their existing positions (i.e., as part of the refutational pretreatment), which McGuire (1964) referred to as intrinsic threat. More often, however, in later inoculation research, perceived threat is established through the use of a forewarning message that signals an impending attack on their current position, referred to as extrinsic threat. Empirical evidence suggests that the addition of a forewarning is more effective in enhancing resistance (McGuire & Papageorgis, 1962). Forewarning can take various formats. For example, in McGuire and Papageorgis (1962), a forewarning was given in the form of an instruction informing the participants that they would be given some messages that attack their beliefs and that they would be asked to report how much the attack messages weakened their beliefs. The basic idea delivered by a forewarning, as Compton (2013) summarized, is that the position one currently holds on to a given issue is likely to face future challenges, which may weaken their conviction regarding that issue.

Evidence suggests that inoculation fails to effectively confer resistance in the absence of perceived threat. For example, Anderson and McGuire (1965) found that the immunizing effects of inoculation were significantly weakened when people were reassured that their peers shared their views. This underscores the central role of perceived threat in the inoculation process, which operates on the premise that individuals have to be supplied with motivation to defend their beliefs (Petty & Cacioppo, 1986), and that this motivation primarily arises from the perception that their beliefs are at risk. Compton and Pfau (2005) correspondingly concluded in their review that inoculation is impossible without threat. Strikingly, however, Banas and Rains (2010) found no significant relationship between perceived threat and resistance in their meta-analysis. This led Banas and Richards (2017) to argue that the traditional operationalization of threat in inoculation research might be flawed. They criticized traditional threat measure – typically asking individuals to rate how harmful and dangerous they found the possibility of encountering opposing arguments (e.g., Burgoon et al., 1978) – for focusing heavily on apprehension, which does not align with the theoretical role of threat in inoculation. Banas and Richards (2017), instead, proposed shifting the focus to motivational threat (i.e., one's motivation to defend their attitude). In their research, motivational threat demonstrated superior criterion, discriminant, and convergent validity than traditional threat measures (Banas & Richards, 2017). In particular, they observed that motivational threat was more strongly associated with resistance than traditional apprehension-based threat.

This re-conceptualization offers a compelling explanation for the nonsignificant findings in Banas and Rains's (2010) meta-analysis. Rather than undermining the importance of threat in inoculation research, Banas and colleagues' work reinforces its essential role, aligning with the conclusions of other researchers regarding the centrality of threat (e.g., Compton & Pfau, 2005; Pfau, 1997). Indeed, Banas and Richards (2017) demonstrated that motivational threat was a significant mediator underlying the effect of inoculation on resistance to counter-persuasion, calling for modeling perceived threat as a part of the resistance-building process, rather than treating it merely as a manipulation check (see also Bessarabova et al., 2024).

Refutational Preemption

A second essential component of a successful inoculation is refutational pre-emption. Refutational preemption "provides specific content that receivers can employ to strengthen attitudes against subsequent change" (Pfau et al., 1997, p. 188). In much of contemporary inoculation research, refutational materials are presented to the participants following the arguments that challenge their current beliefs or attitudes (i.e., counterarguments). In contrast to this passive refutation approach, some earlier research also employed a more active refuta-tion approach where participants were instructed to construct their own refuta-tion materials, such as writing an essay (McGuire & Papageorgis, 1961). Both passive and active refutation approaches have proven effective in conferring resistance, although their relative superiority may vary depending on factors such as the delay between treatment and attack (e.g., Rogers & Thistlethwaite, 1969). Regardless of the format, refutational preemption is believed to serve two main functions: (1) it provides specific arguments that individuals can use to refute future attacks on their attitudes, and (2) it facilitates the process of counterarguing by allowing and encouraging individuals to practice this skill (Compton & Pfau, 2005; Wyer, 1974). The idea of counterarguing here merits some further elaboration. As Compton (2013) noted, counterarguing is concep-tually different from refutation materials in a refutational preemption in that counterarguing involves "the collective generation of counterarguments and refutations, post-inoculation pretreatments" (p. 222). In other words, counter-arguing extends beyond the pretreatment such that individuals who have been successfully inoculated would generate their own arguments against impending attack messages. This cognitive process, motivated by perceived threat, is believed to be key to conferring resistance to counter-influence (Insko, 1967). This explanation has been consistently supported by empirical research (e.g., Pfau & Burgoon, 1988; Pfau et al., 2001).

An extensively studied aspect of refutational pretreatment is the efficacy of different types of refutations, in particular, refutational-same versus -different defense. The core question concerns whether the effectiveness of an inoculation message is limited to only when the attack message makes the same arguments as the ones presented in the refutational preemption. Refutational-same defense raises and refutes the exact arguments that appear in the attack message that an individual later encounters, whereas refutational-different (or -novel) defense preemptively addresses arguments that differ from those employed in the attack message. McGuire (1962) tested these two approaches by exposing participants to an attack message that either repeated the same counterarguments refuted in the inoculation or introduced novel counterarguments. The results suggested that both refutational-same and -different defenses were equally effective in building resistance, with no significant difference in their long-term effectiveness. In their meta-analysis, Banas and Rains (2010) similarly concluded that refutational-same and -different treatments confer equal resistance to counterpersuasion.

This finding has important implications for the practicality of inoculation theory. It means that practitioners do not have to be burdened with developing preemptive messages that capture every single possible attack, which would otherwise seriously limit the theory's real-world application (Pfau & Kenski, 1990). In fact, growing evidence supports that such an umbrella of protection can extend beyond a specific issue to other related topics, offering cross-protection. For example, Parker and colleagues (2012) found that inoculating college students against attacks on their attitudes toward condom use also protected their attitudes toward binge drinking, even though the latter was not mentioned in the message.

The Role of Time

Compton and Pfau (2005) identified two key timing issues in inoculation theory: the time needed for individuals to generate counterarguments (i.e., the optimal amount of time between an inoculation treatment and an attack message) and the duration of protection produced by the inoculation treatment. These two issues jointly determine the ideal time interval between inoculation and attack. The rationale is that, on the one hand, just as a body requires time to develop antibodies after a vaccine, individuals also need time to build cognitive defenses against persuasive attacks (McGuire, 1964); on the other hand, the effects of inoculation, like all message effects, eventually decay. Over time, individuals also experience reduced motivation to generate belief-bolstering materials (Insko, 1967). Thus, finding the right balance is crucial: the interval must allow sufficient time for people to develop resistance while ensuring their motivation to defend their beliefs remains high.

As McGuire (1964) noted, inoculation theory does not prescribe an optimal time interval between treatment and attack; rather, this is an empirical question that can be explored by testing different time delays. Over the years, researchers have examined intervals ranging from immediately after inoculation to several days, weeks, or even months later (for a review, see Compton & Pfau, 2005). The results from these studies vary, leaving the question of optimal timing open. In their meta-analysis, Banas and Rains (2010) hypothesized a curvilinear relationship between inoculation and attack, where a moderate delay would be most effective. However, they found no significant differences in resistance across no delay (i.e., attack immediately after inoculation), moderate delay (i.e., 1–13 days), and long delay (i.e., 14 days or more), although their point estimates did suggest that some decay in resistance for the long-delay group (Banas & Rains, 2010). Although contemporary research commonly employs a two-week delay between treatment and attack (Compton, 2013), the meta-analytic findings challenge the idea of an optimal interval. Banas (2020) argued that this belief is largely influenced by the biological metaphor of inoculation, which breaks down when applied to human cognition. Unlike the biological process where time is needed to build antibodies, the human brain can quickly process information and form judgments, making extended delays unnecessary.

A related point of discussion is the role of reinforcement messages, or boosters. In medical contexts, a booster shot strengthens the protection provided by an initial vaccination. Similarly, it can be expected that a reinforcement message could enhance the resistance developed from an initial inoculation message. Empirical evidence regarding the effectiveness of booster treatments has been mixed. For example, Pfau et al. (1992) observed that reinforcement did not produce a significant additional boost to resistance against smoking onset, a finding echoed by other research indicating limited effectiveness of inoculation in enhancing resistance (e.g., Ivanov et al., 2009; Pfau et al., 2004). However, researchers caution against interpreting these nonsignificant results as definitive evidence against the potential utility of reinforcement. Rather, these findings are believed to reflect challenges in identifying the best timing and format for implementing booster messages (Compton & Pfau, 2005; Ivanov et al., 2009). In support of this perspective, Ivanov et al. (2018) found that booster treatments featuring the original inoculation message – rather than an additional attack message – prolonged attitudinal resistance when presented between the initial inoculation and a final attack. Maertens et al. (2021) observed that regular testing also acted as an effective booster, facilitating the relearning of skills necessary for countering opposing influences. Moreover, Parkers et al. (2022) emphasized that proper timing, rather than frequency, is more impactful in booster message design. Their research identified explicit forewarning as the most effective booster treatment, while the original inoculation message and its refutational preemption were also shown to effectively extend resistance. In summary, boosters hold great potential for enhancing resistance when delivered in the appropriate form and at the right time.

Given the overall strong empirical support for inoculation theory, it is not surprising that it has been applied across a wide variety of contexts. Health, in particular, has seen extensive use of the theory. Inoculation has been used to protect attitudes toward critical health issues such as anti-smoking efforts (e.g., Pfau et al., 1992), condom use (e.g., Parker et al., 2012), and vaccination (e.g.,

Banas et al., 2023). For instance, Pfau and Bockern (1994) applied the theory to help prevent smoking initiation among young adolescents, observing a modest persistence of the initial inoculation effects into the second year. In the political arena, the application of inoculation ranges from protecting candidates from attack messages to sustaining public's attitudes toward specific political issues. One of the earliest studies in this domain by Pfau and Burgoon (1988), for example, found that inoculation effectively conferred resistance to subsequent attack messages among supporters of a candidate, particularly those with strong political identification. A field experiment showed that the inoculation strategy helped mitigate the spiral of silence, enabling inoculated individuals to speak out their political attitudes more freely on contested issues and resist counter-influence (Lin & Pfau, 2007). In commercial communication, inoculation is relevant in settings such as marketing and public relations. For example, inoculation was observed to reduce declines in customer satisfaction following service failures (Mikolon et al., 2015). Ivanov and colleagues (2018) demonstrated that inoculation strategies were more effective than other methods in sustaining positive attitudes toward a destination when faced with negative peer reviews on social media. The breadth and depth of the applications of inoculation extend far beyond these examples. Interested readers can refer to Compton and Pfau (2005) and Ivanov et al. (2020) for a more detailed review. Given our primary focus on the potential of inoculation as a strategy to mitigate misinformation in this Element, we will now shift our attention to its application in this context.

Inoculation and Misinformation Mitigation

With the proliferation of misinformation, psychological inoculation – a theory designed to induce resistance to influence – understandably has gained considerable attention in this context. Indeed, as previously discussed, efforts to debunk or correct misinformation on topics such as climate change and vaccination often fall short of achieving desired outcomes (Chan & Albarracín, 2023; Walter & Tukachinsky, 2020). Sometimes, misinformation continues to shape judgment and decision-making even when people recognize the validity and effectiveness of corrective message (e.g., Thorson, 2016). This continued influence effect is often linked to the structure and functioning of human memory (Seifert, 2002). In many cases, however, especially in real-world scenarios involving misinformation related to science, health, or politics, corrective messages are simply dismissed or rejected by those with entrenched misperceptions. In the previous section, we proposed a biased processing account to explain the denial of corrections, framing corrective messages as a generic type of counter-attitudinal information and viewing misinformation as attitude-consistent information. The resistance to correction, once misinformation has been internalized, highlights the potential effectiveness of a preemptive strategy – also referred to as pre-bunking, in contrast to debunking – designed to prevent the influence of misinformation before it takes hold.

Existing Research on Inoculation against Misinformation

Banas and Miller (2013) were among the first to apply inoculation theory to build resistance against misinformation. Their experiment, which included a control group, an inoculation group, and a metainoculation (i.e., inoculation against inoculation) group, revealed that inoculation effectively fostered resistance to conspiracy theories, while metainoculation diminished its effectiveness. Notably, they also compared the efficacy of fact- versus logic-based inoculation. The fact-based inoculation focused on refuting factual errors in a conspiracy movie, whereas the logic-based approach addressed issues related to parsimony, methodology, and sources of the conspiracy. Their findings indicated that while the fact-based treatment was more effective than the logic-based one, both methods conferred resistance. This study opened new avenues for subsequent research into fact- and logic-based inoculation message design.

One notable example of this research is Cook and colleagues' (2017) study, which examined whether inoculation could effectively neutralize misinformation about climate change presented in the form of false-balance media coverage. In this study, participants were randomly assigned to one of five conditions: a control group, a misinformation attack-only group, a group exposed to a supportive pretreatment followed by the attack message, and two inoculation groups – one receiving a refutational message followed by the attack and the other receiving both a supportive pretreatment and a refutational message prior to the attack. This design largely mirrored an earlier experiment by van der Linden et al. (2017), which also focused on countering climate change misinformation, but differed in the operationalization of inoculation. Van der Linden et al. (2017) employed a traditional approach, using fact-based refutations to challenge counterarguments. Cook et al. (2017), on the other hand, deviated from this approach and used logic-based refutations that questioned the technique and/or reasoning that underlie the misinformation, thereby avoiding the need to pinpoint and reject specific false/misleading claims (Compton et al., 2021). Both studies showed that inoculation effectively preserved positive attitudes toward climate change consensus in the face of misinformation. In a second experiment focused on misinformation involving fake experts questioning expert agreement, Cook et al. (2017) further demonstrated that the logic-based refutation strategy, which explained the flawed reasoning, remained effective in neutralizing the polarizing effects of misinformation. The authors concluded that inoculation might function to enhance strategic monitoring, a state that reduces vulnerability to deception and misinformation.

Recent studies have further expanded this line of research. For example, Maertens et al. (2020) tested whether inoculation could protect attitudes from misinformation over time. They found that while the effect of a consensus message decayed by 48 percent after one week, inoculation produced full protection with a one-week delay between treatment and attack. Vraga et al. (2020) compared the effectiveness of fact- versus logic-based strategies on social media, finding that logic-based approaches were more effective than fact-based approaches in reducing the influence of misinformation, regardless of whether they were placed before or after exposure to misinformation.

While much of the early inoculation research focused on climate change misinformation, its utility in mitigating misinformation has been evidenced across a variety of topics. For example, in the health context, research has shown that inoculation can counter misinformation about COVID-19 vaccines (e.g., Jiang et al., 2022). Comparing a control group, a group receiving supportive messages about vaccines, and an inoculation group exposed to a news article featuring a conspiracy theory that was later refuted, results showed that the inoculation group reported more positive vaccine attitudes and behavioral intentions when presented with misinformation a week later than the supportive-treatment group. In the political realm, Zerback et al. (2021), for example, examined the effect of inoculation against pro-Russian astroturfing comments – comments created by social bots and alike to create the misperception that a given political opinion receives widespread grassroots support). Across three issues, they found that as a form of misinformation, astroturfing comments changed opinions and increased uncertainty. However, inoculation messages using a refutational-same defense successfully built resistance to these comments when they were presented immediately after the treatment. Accordingly, the authors advocated for continuous preemptive efforts utilizing an issue-specific inoculation strategy. Public relations scholars have similarly found inoculation effective against astroturfing attacks on organizational reputation. For example, Boman and Schneider (2021) demonstrated that inoculation outperformed supportive strategies, which reinforce positive attitudes toward the organization, and strategic silence, which involves a lack of communication from the organization, in protecting organizations from misleading attacks.

The findings from various domains have undoubtedly shed light on the utility of inoculation in mitigating misinformation. One important issue that remains undiscussed, however, is the idea of the umbrella of protection generated by inoculation. Recall that in his early research, McGuire (1962) found that resistance could be conferred by both refutational-same and -different defenses. In other words, inoculation protects attitudes even when the counterarguments in attack messages differ from those previously refuted (Banas & Rains, 2010). Further, evidence suggests that inoculation can produce cross-protection, shielding attitudes on related but unmentioned issues from attack (Parker et al., 2012). Can this umbrella of protection extend to misinformation then? This question is crucial given the multifaceted and evolving nature of misinformation, which complicates the development of inoculation messages tailored to each specific narrative. Over the past few years, researchers have sought to answer this by shifting from an argument- or topic-specific approach to what Lewandowsky and van der Linden (2021) described as a "broad-spectrum immunity" strategy. This more generalized approach originated with studies by Banas and Miller (2013) and Cook et al. (2017) and has been significantly expanded by recent research.

The work by Roozenbeek and van der Linden (2019a, 2019b) represents a notable example. The authors developed a game in which players create misinformation and reflect on the techniques to use in its production. This process was designed to put players in the mindset of misinformation creators, encouraging them to actively engage with and think critically about misinformation strategies, ultimately leading to the self-generation of refutations. In doing so, the game apparently employed an active refutation approach (McGuire & Papageorgis, 1961). Participants in the experimental condition were divided into groups and randomly assigned one of four characters, each embodying different motivations for the news articles they produce on immigration. The characters included the denier, who downplays the issue; the alarmist, who exaggerates its severity; the clickbait monger, who focuses on maximizing clicks; and the conspiracy theorist, who aims to undermine trust in official mainstream narratives (Roozenbeek & van der Linden, 2019a). The attack messages were fake news articles on topics related to immigration, employing tactics such as hyperbole, conspiratorial reasoning, and whataboutism. The results of this study showed that compared to a control group, individuals in the experimental group judged the fake news articles as less reliable and persuasive, and indicated lower levels of personal agreement. However, only the difference in perceived reliability was statistically significant. The study also found that the experimental treatment indirectly decreased the perceived persuasiveness of misinformation by lowering its perceived reliability.

In their second study, Roozenbeek and van der Linden (2019b) followed a similar procedure, assigning participants the role of misinformation producers in a game while inoculating them against six specific misinformation tactics during the playtime, including impersonation, use of emotional language, polarization, conspiracy theories, discrediting, and trolling. Using a pre-post design, participants judged the reliability of misinformation in the form of misleading social media posts and news headlines featuring a random sample of the tactics they had been inoculated against, both before and after gameplay. They also evaluated the reliability of two accurate statements, which served a similar function as a control condition. Data from a large convenience sample of over 14,000 participants showed that for each of the misinformation techniques learned in the game, there was a substantial decrease in reliability ratings. In contrast, the change in ratings for the accurate control statements, although significant, was not large enough to be meaningful. Despite some variation across age and political ideology, the inoculation effect was significant across all groups. Combined, these findings suggest that (1) inoculation improves people's awareness of deception strategies, rather than simply making them more skeptical toward all information, and (2) technique-based inoculation can provide broad protection (Roozenbeek & van der Linden, 2019b). These results were further replicated, extended, and supported by multiple studies using different approaches, samples, and time frames (e.g., Basol et al., 2020; Maertens et al., 2021; Roozenbeek et al., 2020, 2021). In addition, the research team launched and tested two additional games aimed respectively at inoculating against COVID-19 misinformation (Basol et al., 2021) and political misinformation during elections (Roozenbeek & van der Linden, 2020).

Lees et al. (2023) similarly developed a gamified inoculation program known as the Spot the Troll Quiz, aimed specifically at equipping individuals with the skills to recognize common tactics employed in online deception. Instead of focusing on misleading content, this program uniquely targets inoculating against trolls or fake profiles on social media platforms. The game features a series of questions, each presenting a social media profile of varying authenticity. Participants must determine which profiles are genuine, guided by tips and contextual information, and receive detailed feedback after submitting their answers. Experimental data indicated that individuals who engaged with the inoculation game demonstrated significantly greater accuracy in discerning troll accounts on Twitter (now X) compared to a control group. In addition, they rated fake news headlines as less reliable, exhibiting a notable cross-protection effect. Importantly, the program proved equally effective across age groups, benefiting both older and younger adults, as well as individuals of different party identification, including Republicans and Democrats.

A closely related approach to broad-spectrum inoculation is illustrated by Roozenbeek et al. (2022). Instead of using games to encourage active refutations, this work employed short intervention videos, aligning with a passive refutation strategy. The researchers developed five inoculation videos, each explaining a common rhetorical device used in online misinformation, including (1) ad hominem attacks that attack individuals rather than address their arguments, (2) emotional language aimed at evoking emotions such as fear or outrage, (3) false dichotomies that present limited, mutually exclusive options, (4) incoherent arguments, and (5) scapegoating, which singles out and blames a person or group for a problem. All videos followed a similar structure: a forewarning informing people of an impending misinformation attack, followed by a refutational preemption of the manipulation technique with a weakened example featuring the technique. The study involved five lab experiments testing the effectiveness of each video. Participants were randomly assigned to watch either an intervention or control video, then rated ten social media posts adapted from real-world examples that were either neutral or manipulative. On average, each participant rated five neutral posts and five manipulative ones. Across four outcome measures, including the ability to recognize manipulation techniques, confidence in their recognition ability, ability to distinguish between trustworthy and untrustworthy content, and the quality of sharing decisions, the inoculation group outperformed the control group in 80 percent of the cases. In addition, there were no consistent interactions between the experimental condition and individual difference variables such as political ideology or analytical thinking, demonstrating the robustness of inoculation's effects across different populations. A sixth study was done to rule out possible order effects, followed by a large-scale field study on YouTube with the two videos on emotional language use and false dichotomies. The experimental group watched one of the videos as a YouTube ad. A random 30 percent of the group was then displayed a single-item question designed to test their ability to identify the manipulation technique within twenty-four hours after watching the ad. Compared to the control group, the experimental group showed significantly better recognition, although the effect size fell below the preregistered smallest effect of interest. Collectively, the findings of these studies suggest that inoculation against the manipulation techniques underlying misinformation can effectively provide broad-spectrum immunity to misinformation (Lewandowsky & Van Der Linden, 2021).

To summarize, inoculation against the persuasive effects of misinformation involves two key components: (1) a forewarning about the prevalence of misinformation in the media landscape and its potential to undermine one's attitudes and beliefs, and (2) refutations that address the arguments and/or manipulation tactics used in misinformation, highlighting how to identify, expose, and counter these weaknesses and fallacies. This approach helps individuals to develop better abilities and motivation to identify and resist subsequent misinformation across diverse domains (for a meta-analysis, see Lu et al., 2023).

In the traditional inoculation paradigm, it is crucial that this strategy is implemented before individuals are exposed to misinformation. However, recent theoretical development of inoculation suggests that therapeutic inoculation (as opposed to conventional prophylactic inoculation) may also prove effective. Next, we briefly discuss the concept of therapeutic inoculation and its relevance to mitigating misinformation.

Therapeutic (versus Prophylactic) Inoculation in Misinformation Context

An assumption that has been at the root of psychological inoculation theory for years is that, analogous to vaccines in a medical context, inoculation is a preventative treatment intended to be administered before an attack that could change an existing position. Indeed, McGuire (1964) started his series of experiments with an exclusive focus on cultural truisms to be consistent with the reasoning of this analogy. At the core of this assumption is the notion that there must be a desired state or a preferred position on an issue. However, an influence attempt can still take place without such desired state or preferred position (e.g., to create a new attitude) and inoculation can be implemented to pre-empt such influence attempts. Compton (2020) gave a detailed explanation of this logic, noting its relevance to conventional prophylactic inoculations designed to protect individuals in a desired state from potential changes. Compton (2020), however, also emphasized the importance of considering alternative forms of inoculation, such as therapeutic inoculations.

Just as vaccines can be therapeutic and administered to people who are already infected to reduce the harm of a disease, psychological inoculation may also be provided to those who already hold misconceptions (Compton & Pfau, 2005). Wood (2007) empirically tested this idea. Focusing on agricultural biotechnology as the main topic, Wood (2007) recruited participants who were supportive, neutral, and opposed to biotech crops and randomly assigned them to either a treatment or a control group. The inoculation message presented to the treatment group included a forewarning about the pervasiveness of arguments opposing biotech, along with specific counterarguments against biotech that were raised and refuted. All participants were then exposed to an attack message using the same previously refuted arguments. Results showed that, compared to their counterparts in the control condition, those with initially neutral and opposing positions who received the inoculation message perceived a higher level of threat. In addition, those with supportive and neutral positions engaged in greater counterarguing. Importantly, regardless of the prior stance, all individuals in the inoculation condition reported a more positive attitude post-attack than those in the control condition. It is especially worth noting that the inoculated participants who initially opposed biotech did not demonstrate any backfire effect; rather, this group was the only one to show an increase in positive attitudes. Similar patterns were observed by Ivanov et al. (2017), who found that inoculation shifted neutral and opposing attitudes in the desired direction and helped sustain these attitude gains in the face of an attack message.

One potential issue in therapeutic inoculation lies in the fact that the inoculation effects might be empirically confounded with therapeutic effects. This might be particularly true for psychological inoculation – the confounding of generic message effects and inoculation effects means the loss of scientific precision, although it might not be an issue from the practical point of view. Systematic theorizing regarding the effects of therapeutic inoculations remains underdeveloped. For example, it is still unclear how an attitude-consistent message – such as that used in a therapeutic inoculation administered to an opposing individual – elicits a sense of threat, whether threat is what drives resistance in therapeutic inoculation, and, if not, what alternative mechanisms might be at play (Compton, 2020). Indeed, empirical evidence suggests that (apprehension-based) threat does not account for the efficacy of therapeutic inoculation, with perceived credibility and motivational threat proposed as potential alternative explanations (e.g., Ivanov et al., 2022; see also Mason et al., 2024). These unsolved theoretical questions, however, should not discourage its use in practice, given the robust empirical evidence. In fact, several studies we reviewed above that specifically addressed the context of misinformation also provide some evidence, albeit in a less direct manner, supporting the utility of therapeutic inoculations. One such example is the van der Linden et al. (2017) study, which tested the effectiveness of inoculation treatments on the topic of climate change among individuals who self-identified as Democrats, Independents, and Republicans. They found a highly similar pattern, with the inoculation treatment successfully preserving comparable proportions of attitude gains across all three groups. This observation was replicated by Williams and Bond (2020) and Maertens et al. (2020). Compton et al. (2021) suspected that the key to those results lies in how inoculation increases awareness of attitude vulnerabilities and facilitates more strategic monitoring (see also the discussion in Lewandowsky & van der Linden, 2021). In sum, it seems that inoculation does not necessarily have to precede exposure to misinformation and the development of misconceptions to be effective, although the likelihood (and ease) of "completely curing" an individual is presumably greater when it does.

From Individuals to Communities

In a *Science* commentary, van der Linden et al. (2017) brought up the notion that one of the important but underexplored benefits of inoculation is its potential to spread, allowing for societal-level resistance against misinformation through interpersonal communication. The metaphor of "herd immunity" has been used to elaborate on this idea: pretty much in the same way as the spread of a virus is curtailed when a critical portion of the population becomes immune to a disease, the spread of misinformation could be similarly controlled if a large enough segment of the population is inoculated against it (Lewandowsky & van der Linden, 2021). A key mechanism for achieving such cognitive herd immunity lies in interpersonal talk, more specifically, post-inoculation discussions. This relies on at least two conditions: (1) inoculation must encourage interpersonal talk, and (2) interpersonal talk should change attitudes or beliefs in the desired direction. Research supports both of these conditions.

On the first front, multiple studies have shown that inoculation can disrupt the spiral of silence surrounding contested issues, increasing individuals' willingness to publicly express their attitudes and beliefs on these issues (e.g., Lin & Pfau, 2007; Lin, 2022). In addition, Ivanov et al. (2012) theorized that interpersonal, vocalized counterarguing, alongside internal, subvocal counterarguing, following inoculation could not only bolster resistance to attacks but also help spread the inoculation message across social networks. In line with this, they found that inoculated individuals engaged in more interpersonal conversations about the issue compared to those not exposed to the inculcation message, and these conversations further strengthened resistance to subsequent attacks. In a later study, Ivanov et al. (2012) took a closer look at the content of post-inoculation conversations. They observed that inoculated individuals were more likely to engage in post-inoculation talk for advocacy purposes than those in the control group. People who were inoculated were more likely to share arguments from the inoculation message, introduce novel issue-relevant arguments, and discuss related topics. They were also more likely to encounter challenges from their conversation partners. These findings offer insights into how inoculation effects might be disseminated through social networks (see also Ivanov et al., 2018).

Does post-inoculation talk actually change the conversation partners' attitudes or beliefs then? While direct empirical evidence is limited, decades of research on the effects of campaign-induced interpersonal communication offer useful insights. This line of work highlights the role of interpersonal talk in shaping health campaign outcomes. Specifically, it is believed that mass media campaigns can spark interpersonal conversations, which in turn lead to attitude and behavioral changes (Dillard et al., 2022; Southwell & Yzer, 2007). In a meta-analysis, Jeong and Bae (2018) confirmed that campaign-induced conversations had a significant positive impact on campaign-targeted health outcomes. That is, compared to when conversations were absent, the odds of achieving campaign goals were significantly higher when campaign-induced interpersonal communication occurred. This finding underscores the persuasive power of interpersonal talk. To the extent that post-inoculation talk can be viewed as a special case of campaign-induced interpersonal communication, it likely holds similar potential to spread protection and foster societal-level resistance to misinformation.

Designing Inoculation Messages against Misinformation

It should be clear at this point that psychological inoculation offers a flexible, effective tool for combating misinformation. In concluding this section, we now turn to the design of inoculation messages against misinformation. At the broadest level, as with any persuasive communication program, successful implementation of an inoculation intervention requires clearly defined goals and target audiences, as well as thoughtful message development, testing, and execution. These are often achieved through a multi-stage process that involves planning and strategy development, developing and pretesting messages and materials, implementation, and effectiveness assessment and program refinement (National Cancer Institute, 2004). Formative research, in particular, plays a crucial role in this process, helping to determine the optimal approaches concerning the selection of messages, sources, and communication channels for a specific group of target audiences (Atkin & Freimuth, 2013). Essentially, through formative research, practitioners can identify elements that work best and avoid those that may be counter-productive in relation to the characteristics of their intended audience.

Specific to the design of inoculation messages, a good example is the inclusion of emotional content. Nabi (2003) found that inoculation messages with a more consistent distribution of emotionally evocative visuals generally conferred greater resistance to attacks. Connecting message content with characteristics of the recipients, Ivanov et al. (2009) observed that the effectiveness of cognitive versus affective inoculation content depended on individuals' attitude base: cognitive inoculation messages were more successful at conferring resistance to attacks when delivered to people who primarily had a cognitive-based attitude, whereas emotional inoculation messages were more effective for those whose attitude base was primarily affective. This suggests that inoculation messages are most effective when their content matches the audience's attitude base, although there is also evidence that a combination of cognitive and affective content performs equally well in defending against multiple attacks (Ivanov et al., 2012). Thorough formative research is essential for determining the most suitable message content for the audience and situation.

Equally important is the identification and revision of any unproductive components of inoculation messages. For example, inoculation may trigger reactance in recipients, which further reduces the effectiveness of the treatment (Szabo & Pfau, 2001). Reactance, defined as "the motivational state that is hypothesized to occur when a freedom is eliminated or threatened with elimination" (Brehm & Brehm, 1981, p. 37), manifests as a combination of anger and critical cognitions (Dillard & Shen, 2005). Given the long-observed negative impact of reactance on persuasive outcomes, it is crucial that inoculation messages are constructed in ways that avoid eliciting reactance to the treatment itself. Instead, some researchers have sought to harness reactance by directing it toward the threat or attack, leveraging its motivational property to enhance the inoculation effect (Miller et al., 2013). Additionally, research by Richards and colleagues has investigated how inoculation can reduce reactance to freedom-threatening messages. Their findings suggest that individuals can be inoculated against reactance (e.g., Richards & Banas, 2015), particularly those who are high in trait reactance (Richards et al., 2021). However, they caution against using high-threat inoculation – particularly apprehension-based threats – when aiming to mitigate reactance (Richards & Banas, 2018; Richards et al., 2017). Notably, the message design in these studies tends to be an instruction for individuals not to let reactance be their response – which takes the form of a request, an influence attempt, or a generic persuasive message, rather than an inoculation message. Conceptually, psychological reactance arises within the individual, while the target of (medical and psychological) inoculation is external to the individual's body (e.g., a virus) or mind (e.g., an influence attempt). Hence, there is a loss of scientific precision here. Overall, empirical evidence for the idea of inoculation against psychological reactance remains inconclusive. Again, formative research, including both preproduction and production testing, is vital for ensuring that the message achieves its intended effect while minimizing unintended consequences.

Finally, we consider the specific components of an inoculation message. Recall that two key constructs underlying the effectiveness of (prophylactic) inoculation are threat and refutational preemption. Although one may perceive threat merely by being exposed to arguments that challenge their existing position – a key aspect of refutational preemption (McGuire, 1964), research suggests that an explicit forewarning message informing individuals of an impending attack tends to be more effective. Such forewarnings help individuals recognize the vulnerability of their positions and ultimately enhance their resistance (McGuire & Papageorgis, 1962). Thus, a crucial first step in designing an inoculation message is often to develop an effective forewarning. There are, however, exceptions. For example, Ivanov (2017) suggested that explicit forewarning can be omitted in therapeutic inoculation situations where inoculation aims to "cure" rather than solely "prevent." In these cases, forewarnings may seem irrelevant and nonsensical for individuals who do not currently hold a desirable or correct position. The second key component, refutational preemption, involves presenting a weakened form of counterarguments and/or manipulation techniques commonly used in misinformation, followed by refutations of these arguments or techniques. The weakened arguments often rely on anecdotal stories, testimonials, or problematic evidence and logic (Ivanov, 2017). After this, individuals can either be given refutational material containing strong evidence and facts, as in a passive refutation approach, or be instructed to develop their own rebuttals, as in an active refutation approach. Of course, as new technologies are increasingly integrated into the delivery of intervention programs, we are no longer limited to message-based inoculations. This evolution is exemplified by the gamified inoculation designed by Roozenbeek and van der Linden (2019a, 2019b). Nonetheless, the underlying components and logic of the design remain consistent.

4 Conclusion

Misinformation is here to stay without effective interventions. Over the past decade, society as a whole has collectively grappled with its sociopolitical consequences across all domains. Health misinformation, in particular, exacerbated by a global pandemic, has had devastating effects, including loss of life. Efforts to correct misinformation repeatedly fall short of achieving desirable effects (Chan & Albarracín, 2023). Worse still, correction attempts can sometimes backfire, reinforcing false beliefs instead (Chan et al., 2017; Nyhan & Reifler, 2010). This Element aims to provide a framework for understanding the persistence of misinformation and the lack of ideal effects from corrections. We view corrective information as a special case of counter-attitudinal information and misinformation as attitude-congruent information. That is, for individuals who have adopted a misinformed position, subsequent corrective information runs counter to their existing beliefs, while misinformation aligns with them. From the perspective of social judgment theory (Sherif et al. 1965), counter-attitudinal corrective messages typically fall within an individual's latitude of rejection, making them unlikely to persuade and potentially leading to greater entrenchment of misconceptions. Cognitive dissonance theory (Festinger, 1957) suggests that the psychological discomfort caused by counter-attitudinal corrections may lead individuals to dismiss or reject them to alleviate cognitive dissonance. Misinformation, on the other hand, is consistent with their pre-existing beliefs, prompting more favorable responses. Within the framework of motivated information processing (Chaiken et al., 1996), when people prioritize motivations other than accuracy – such as defense motivation, which is often the case with misinformation (Walter & Murphy, 2018) – biased responses occur, leading them to selectively engage with information in ways that reinforce their pre-existing attitudes. This means negative responses to corrective messages, such as inattentiveness and counterarguing, and acceptance of misinformation. Collectively, these theoretical frameworks provide useful lenses for understanding the persistence of misinformation as biased processing guided by pre-existing beliefs.

Empirically, we reviewed data from two studies examining the mechanisms underlying the persistence of misinformation on climate change and vaccination, respectively (Shen & Zhou, 2021; Zhou & Shen, 2022). The findings from both studies demonstrated a robust biased processing pattern where message type (i.e., scientific/corrective message versus misinformation) and pre-existing position interacted to shape source and message perceptions and processing. People with misinformed beliefs assessed corrective messages more negatively and misinformation more positively, and their biased evaluation was more extreme than those with a correct prior position. In addition, it appears that misinformation operates through a more superficial, automatic process; scientific information, on the other hand, influences primarily via a deeper, more effortful cognitive process. This cognitive engagement requires both the ability and the (accuracy) motivation – qualities that misinformation believers often lack. Lastly, testing a model of misinformation persistence, our data confirmed that biased cognitions, as reflected in source and message perceptions, underlie and explain the effects of misinformation and corrective information on polarized attitudes and policy preferences. Moreover, these biased source and message perceptions drive information-seeking behaviors and public deliberation engagement in ways that contribute to polarization and extremism.

Misinformation persists despite correction as a result of biased processing means that instead of debunking misinformation after it has taken root as misconceptions, we may benefit from something more preemptive in nature that allows pre-bunking. Psychological inoculation theory (McGuire, 1964) has emerged as a promising strategy for mitigating misinformation (van der Linden et al., 2017). Inoculation operates through two key mechanisms: first, by creating a perceived threat that raises awareness of the vulnerability of one's beliefs, motivating individuals to defend those beliefs; and second, through counterarguing, which involves generating counterarguments against anticipated misinformation. This process ultimately confers resistance to subsequent attempts to mislead. A substantial body of research has yielded empirical evidence supporting the effectiveness of inoculation in inducing resistance to misinformation across diverse contexts (e.g., Boman, 2023; Maertens et al., 2020; Roozenbeek et al., 2022; Spampatti et al., 2024; van der Linden et al., 2017). In addition, consistent with the results from earlier research on the effectiveness of refutational-different defense (e.g., McGuire, 1962), the findings of these studies suggest that inoculation – especially when it is focused on manipulation techniques commonly used in misinformation rather than specific arguments – can offer broad-spectrum protection against misinformation (e.g., Cook et al., 2017; Roozenbeek & van der Linden, 2019b). Another promising insight from this research is the potential of therapeutic inoculation: it may help "cure" individuals whose attitudes or beliefs are not in a desired state to begin with (van der Linden et al., 2017; Williams & Bond, 2020).

Psychological inoculation is of pivotal relevance to the ongoing battle against misinformation. The robust scholarship to date has not only shed light on the efficacy of inoculation-based interventions but also built a solid foundation for future research to continue exploring their potential for building endurable societal resistance to misinformation. Theoretical and empirical questions concerning therapeutic inoculation, post-inoculation discussions, and the timing of treatment delivery, among others, remain exciting avenues for further inquiry. By unpacking the nuances and complexities of inoculation, we will be better empowered to develop a comprehensive defense against the pervasive threat of misinformation and navigate the intricate informational landscape. This, in turn, equips us to address the challenges posed by unprecedented social polarization and division, ultimately fostering a more informed and cohesive society.

References

Adams, Z., Osman, M., Bechlivanidis, C., & Meder, B. (2023). (Why) is misinformation a problem? *Perspectives on Psychological Science, 18*(6), 1436–1463. https://doi.org/10.1177/17456916221141344.

Ahluwalia, R. (2000). Examination of psychological processes underlying resistance to persuasion. *Journal of Consumer Research, 27*(2), 217–232. https://doi.org/10.1086/314321.

Allcott, H., & Gentzkow, M. (2017). Social media and fake news in the 2016 election. *Journal of Economic Perspectives, 31*(2), 211–236. https://doi.org/10.1257/jep.31.2.211.

Amin, A. B., Bednarczyk, R. A., Ray, C. E. et al. (2017). Association of moral values with vaccine hesitancy. *Nature Human Behaviour, 1*(12), 873–880. https://doi.org/10.1038/s41562-017-0256-5.

Anderson, L. R., & McGuire, W. J. (1965). Prior reassurance of group consensus as a factor in producing resistance to persuasion. *Sociometry, 28*(1), 44–56. https://doi.org/10.2307/2786084.

Atkin, C. K., & Freimuth, V. (2013). Guidelines for formative evaluation research in campaign design. In R. E. Rice & C. K. Atkin (Eds.), *Public communication campaigns* (Vol. 4, pp. 53–68). SAGE.

Balmas, M. (2014). When fake news becomes real: Combined exposure to multiple news sources and political attitudes of inefficacy, alienation, and cynicism. *Communication Research, 41*(3), 430–454. https://doi.org/10.1177/0093650212453600.

Banas, J. A. (2020). Inoculation theory. In J. Van den Bulck, D. R. Ewoldsen, M.-L. Mares, & E. Scharrer (Eds.), *International encyclopedia of media psychology* (pp. 1–8). John Wiley & Sons. https://doi.org/10.1002/9781119011071.iemp0285.

Banas, J. A., Bessarabova, E., Penkauskas, M. C., & Talbert, N. (2023). Inoculating against anti-vaccination conspiracies. *Health Communication, 39*(9), 1760–1768. https://doi.org/10.1080/10410236.2023.2235733.

Banas, J. A., & Miller, G. (2013). Inducing resistance to conspiracy theory propaganda: Testing inoculation and metainoculation strategies. *Human Communication Research, 39*(2), 184–207. https://doi.org/10.1111/hcre.12000.

Banas, J. A., & Rains, S. A. (2010). A meta-analysis of research on inoculation theory. *Communication Monographs, 77*(3), 281–311. https://doi.org/10.1080/03637751003758193.

Banas, J. A., & Richards, A. S. (2017). Apprehension or motivation to defend attitudes? Exploring the underlying threat mechanism in inoculation-induced resistance to persuasion. *Communication Monographs*, *84*(2), 164–178. https://doi.org/10.1080/03637751.2017.1307999.

Basol, M., Roozenbeek, J., Berriche, M. et al. (2021). Towards psychological herd immunity: Cross-cultural evidence for two prebunking interventions against COVID-19 misinformation. *Big Data & Society*, *8*(1), 205395172110138. https://doi.org/10.1177/20539517211013868.

Basol, M., Roozenbeek, J., & Van der Linden, S. (2020). Good news about bad news: Gamified inoculation boosts confidence and cognitive immunity against fake news. *Journal of Cognition*, *3*(1), 2. https://doi.org/10.5334/joc.91.

Beauvois, J. L., & Joule, R. (1996). *A radical dissonance theory.* Taylor & Francis.

Bessarabova, E., Banas, J. A., Reinikainen, H. et al. (2024). Assessing inoculation's effectiveness in motivating resistance to conspiracy propaganda in Finnish and United States samples. *Frontiers in Psychology*, *15*, 1416722. https://doi.org/10.3389/fpsyg.2024.1416722.

Boman, C. D. (2023). Protecting against disinformation: Using inoculation to cultivate reactance toward astroturf attacks. *Journal of Public Relations Research*, *35*, 162–181. https://doi.org/10.1080/1062726X.2023.2195184.

Boman, C. D., & Schneider, E. J. (2021). Finding an antidote: Testing the use of proactive crisis strategies to protect organizations from astroturf attacks. *Public Relations Review*, *47*(1), 102004. https://doi.org/10.1016/j.pubrev.2020.102004.

Brannon, L. A., Tagler, M. J., & Eagly, A. H. (2007). The moderating role of attitude strength in selective exposure to information. *Journal of Experimental Social Psychology*, *43*(4), 611–617. https://doi.org/10.1016/j.jesp.2006.05.001.

Brehm J. W., & Brehm S. S. (1981). *Psychological reactance: A theory of freedom and control.* Academic Press.

Burgoon, M., Cohen, M., Miller, M. D., & Montgomery, C. L. (1978). An empirical test of a model of resistance to persuasion. *Human Communication Research*, *5*(1), 27–39. https://doi.org/10.1111/j.1468-2958.1978.tb00620.x.

Carrasco-Farre, C. (2022). The fingerprints of misinformation: How deceptive content differs from reliable sources in terms of cognitive effort and appeal to emotions. *Humanities and Social Sciences Communications*, *9*(1), 1–18. https://doi.org/10.1057/s41599-022-01174-9.

Chaiken, S. (1987). The heuristic model of persuasion. In M. P. Zanna, J. M. Olson, & C. P. Herman (Eds.), *Social influence: The Ontario symposium* (Vol.5, pp. 3–39). Lawrence Erlbaum Associates.

Chaiken, S., Giner-Sorolla, R., & Chert, S. (1996). Beyond accuracy: Defense and impression motives in heuristic and systematic information processing. In P. M. Gollwitzer & J. A. Bargh (Eds.), *The psychology of action: Linking cognition and motivation to behavior* (pp. 553–578). Guilford Press.

Chaiken, S., Liberman, A., & Eagly, A. H. (1989). Heuristic and systematic processing within and beyond the persuasion context. In J. S. Uleman & J. A. Bargh (Eds.), *Unintended thought* (pp. 212–252). Guilford Press.

Chan, J. C. K., O'Donnell, R., & Manley, K. D. (2022). Warning weakens retrieval-enhanced suggestibility only when it is given shortly after misinformation: The critical importance of timing. *Journal of Experimental Psychology: Applied, 28*(4), 694–716. https://doi.org/10.1037/xap0000394.

Chan, M. P. S., & Albarracín, D. (2023). A meta-analysis of correction effects in science-relevant misinformation. *Nature Human Behaviour, 7*(9), 1514–1525. https://doi.org/10.1038/s41562-023-01623-8.

Chan, M. P. S., Jones, C. R., Hall Jamieson, K., & Albarracín, D. (2017). Debunking: A meta-analysis of the psychological efficacy of messages countering misinformation. *Psychological Science, 28*(11), 1531–1546. https://doi.org/10.1177/0956797617714579.

Chen, S., & Chaiken, S. (1999). The heuristic-systematic model in its broader context. In S. Chaiken & Y. Trope (Eds.), *Dual-process theories in social psychology* (pp.73–96). Guilford Press.

Chen, L., & Tang, H. (2023). Examining the persuasion process of narrative fear appeals on health misinformation correction. *Information, Communication & Society, 26*(15), 2923–2941. https://doi.org/10.1080/1369118x.2022.2128849.

Compton, J. (2013). Inoculation theory. In J. P. Dillard & L. Shen (Eds.), *The Sage handbook of persuasion: Developments in theory and practice* (2nd ed., pp. 220–236). Sage.

Compton, J. (2020). Prophylactic versus therapeutic inoculation treatments for resistance to influence. *Communication Theory, 30*(3), 330–343. https://doi.org/10.1093/ct/qtz004.

Compton, J. A., & Pfau, M. (2005). Inoculation theory of resistance to influence at maturity: Recent progress in theory development and application and suggestions for future research. *Annals of the International Communication Association, 29*(1), 97–146. https://doi.org/10.1080/23808985.2005.11679045.

Compton, J., van der Linden, S., Cook, J., & Basol, M. (2021). Inoculation theory in the post-truth era: Extant findings and new frontiers for contested science, misinformation, and conspiracy theories. *Social and Personality Psychology Compass, 15*(6), e12602. https://doi.org/10.1111/spc3.12602.

Connor Desai, S., & Reimers, S. (2023). Does explaining the origins of misinformation improve the effectiveness of a given correction? *Memory & Cognition, 51*(2), 422–436. https://doi.org/10.3758/s13421-022-01354-7.

Cook, J. (2019). Understanding and countering misinformation about climate change. In I. Chiluwa & S. Samoilenko (Eds.), *Handbook of research on deception, fake news, and misinformation online* (pp. 281–306). IGI-Global.

Cook, J., Lewandowsky, S., & Ecker, U. K. H. (2017). Neutralizing misinformation through inoculation: Exposing misleading argumentation techniques reduces their influence. *PloS One, 12*(5), e0175799. https://doi.org/10.1371/journal.pone.0175799.

Cornwell, J. F. M., & Higgins, E. T. (2018). The tripartite motivational human essence: Value, control, and truth working together. In M. van Zomeren & J. F. Dovidio (Eds.), *The Oxford handbook of the human essence* (pp. 71–81). Oxford University Press.

Denner, N., Viererbl, B., & Koch, T. (2023). Effects of repeated corrections of misinformation on organizational trust: More is not always better. *International Journal of Strategic Communication, 17*(1), 39–53. https://doi.org/10.1080/1553118x.2022.2135098.

Dillard, J. P., Li, S. S., & Cannava, K. (2022). Talking about sugar-sweetened beverages: Causes, processes, and consequences of campaign-induced interpersonal communication. *Health Communication, 37*(3), 316–326. https://doi.org/10.1080/10410236.2020.1838107.

Dillard, J. P., & Shen, L. (2005). On the nature of reactance and its role in persuasive health communication. *Communication Monographs, 72*(2), 144–168. https://doi.org/10.1080/03637750500111815.

Dillard, J. P., Shen, L., & Vail, R. G. (2007). Does perceived message effectiveness cause persuasion or vice versa? 17 consistent answers. *Human Communication Research, 33*(4), 467–488. https://doi.org/10.1111/j.1468-2958.2007.00308.x.

Dillingham, L. L., & Ivanov, B. (2016). Using postinoculation talk to strengthen generated resistance. *Communication Research Reports, 33*(4), 295–302. https://doi.org/10.1080/08824096.2016.1224161.

Ecker, U. K. H., Lewandowsky, S., Chang, E. P., & Pillai, R. (2014). The effects of subtle misinformation in news headlines. *Journal of Experimental Psychology: Applied, 20*(4), 323–335. https://doi.org/10.1037/xap0000028.

Ecker, U. K., Lewandowsky, S., Cook, J. et al. (2022). The psychological drivers of misinformation belief and its resistance to correction. *Nature Reviews Psychology, 1*(1), 13–29. https://doi.org/10.1038/s44159-021-00006-y.

Ecker, U. K., Lewandowsky, S., Jayawardana, K., & Mladenovic, A. (2019). Refutations of equivocal claims: No evidence for an ironic effect of counter-argument number. *Journal of Applied Research in Memory and Cognition, 8* (1), 98–107. https://doi.org/10.1016/j.jarmac.2018.07.005.

Ecker, U. K. H., Lewandowsky, S., & Tang, D. T. W. (2010). Explicit warnings reduce but do not eliminate the continued influence of misinformation. *Memory & Cognition, 38*(8), 1087–1100. https://doi.org/10.3758/mc.38.8.1087.

Enders, A., Farhart, C., Miller, J. et al. (2023). Are Republicans and conservatives more likely to believe conspiracy theories? *Political Behavior, 45,* 2001–2024. https://doi.org/10.1007/s11109-022-09812-3.

Fazio, R. H. (2007). Attitudes as object–evaluation associations of varying strength. *Social Cognition, 25*(5), 603–637. https://doi.org/10.1521/soco .2007.25.5.603.

Festinger, L. (1957). *A theory of cognitive dissonance.* Stanford University Press.

Fishbein, M., & Ajzen, I. (2010). *Predicting and changing behavior: The reasoned action approach.* Psychology Press.

Fombonne, E., Goin-Kochel, R. P., O'Roak, B. J. et al. (2020). Beliefs in vaccine as causes of autism among SPARK cohort caregivers. *Vaccine, 38* (7), 1794–1803. https://doi.org/10.1016/j.vaccine.2019.12.026.

Garrett, R. K., & Stroud, N. J. (2014). Partisan paths to exposure diversity: Differences in pro-and counterattitudinal news consumption. *Journal of Communication, 64*(4), 680–701. https://doi.org/10.1111/jcom.12105.

Giner-Sorolila, R., & Chaiken, S. (1997). Selective use of heuristic and systematic processing under defense motivation. *Personality and Social Psychology Bulletin, 23*(1), 84–97. https://doi.org/10.1177/0146167297231009.

Guess, A. M., & Lyons, B. A. (2020). Misinformation, disinformation, and online propaganda. In N. Persily & J. A. Tucker (Eds.), *Social media and democracy: The state of the field, prospects for reform* (pp. 10–33). Cambridge University Press.

Gunther, A. C., McLaughlin, B., Gotlieb, M. R., & Wise, D. (2017). Who says what to whom: Content versus source in the hostile media effect. *International Journal of Public Opinion Research, 29*(3), 363–383. https://doi.org/10.1093/ijpor/edw009.

Hameleers, M. (2022). Separating truth from lies: Comparing the effects of news media literacy interventions and fact-checkers in response to political misinformation in the US and Netherlands. *Information, Communication & Society, 25*(1), 110–126. https://doi.org/10.1080/1369118x.2020.1764603.

Harmon-Jones, E., & Mills, J. (2019). An introduction to cognitive dissonance theory and an overview of current perspectives on the theory. In E. Harmon-

Jones (Ed.), *Cognitive dissonance: Reexamining a pivotal theory in psychology* (2nd ed., pp. 3–24). American Psychological Association.

Hart, P. S., & Nisbet, E. C. (2012). Boomerang effects in science communication: How motivated reasoning and identity cues amplify opinion polarization about climate mitigation policies. *Communication Research, 39*(6), 701–723. https://doi.org/10.1177/0093650211416646.

Heider, F. (1946). Attitudes and cognitive organization. *The Journal of Psychology, 21*(1), 107–112. https://doi.org/10.1080/00223980.1946.9917275.

Higgins, E. T. (1996). Knowledge activation: Accessibility, applicability, and salience. In E. T. Higgins & A. W. Kruglanski (Eds.), *Social psychology: Handbook of basic principles* (pp. 133–168). Guilford.

Insko, C. A. (1967). *Theories of attitude change.* Appleton-Century-Crofts.

Ivanov, B. (2017). *Inoculation theory applied in health and risk messaging.* Oxford research encyclopedia of communication.

Ivanov, B., Dillingham, L. L., Parker, K. A. et al. (2018). Sustainable attitudes: Protecting tourism with inoculation messages. *Annals of Tourism Research, 73,* 26–34. https://doi.org/10.1016/j.annals.2018.08.006.

Ivanov, B., Parker, K. A., & Dillingham, L. L. (2020). Inoculation theory as a strategic tool. In H. D. O'Hair & M. J. O'Hair (Eds.), *Handbook of applied communication research* (Vol.1, pp. 13–28). Wiley.

Ivanov, B., Parker, K. A., & Pfau, M. (2012). The interaction effect of attitude base and multiple attacks on the effectiveness of inoculation. *Communication Research Reports, 29*(1), 1–11. https://doi.org/10.1080/08824096.2011.616789.

Ivanov, B., Pfau, M., & Parker, K. A. (2009). Can inoculation withstand multiple attacks? An examination of the effectiveness of the inoculation strategy compared to the supportive and restoration strategies. *Communication Research, 36*(5), 655–676. https://doi.org/10.1177/0093650209338909.

Ivanov, B., Rains, S. A., Dillingham, L. L. et al. (2022). The role of threat and counterarguing in therapeutic inoculation. *Southern Communication Journal, 87*(1), 15–27. https://doi.org/10.1080/1041794X.2021.1983012.

Ivanov, B., Rains, S. A., Geegan, S. A. et al. (2017). Beyond simple inoculation: Examining the persuasive value of inoculation for audiences with initially neutral or opposing attitudes. *Western Journal of Communication, 81*(1), 105–126. https://doi.org/10.1080/10570314.2016.1224917.

Ivanov, B., Sellnow, T., Getchell, M., & Burns, W. (2018). The potential for inoculation messages and postinoculation talk to minimize the social impact of politically motivated acts of violence. *Journal of Contingencies and Crisis Management, 26*(4), 414–424. https://doi.org/10.1111/1468-5973.12213.

Ivanov, B., Sims, J. D., Compton, J. et al. (2015). The general content of postinoculation talk: Recalled issue-specific conversations following inoculation treatments. *Western Journal of Communication, 79*(2), 218–238. https://doi.org/10.1080/10570314.2014.943423.

Janmohamed, K., Walter, N., Nyhan, K. et al. (2021). Interventions to mitigate COVID-19 misinformation: A systematic review and meta-analysis. *Journal of Health Communication, 26*(12), 846–857. https://doi.org/10.1080/10810730.2021.2021460.

Jeong, M., & Bae, R. E. (2018). The effect of campaign-generated interpersonal communication on campaign-targeted health outcomes: A meta-analysis. *Health Communication, 33*(8), 988–1003. https://doi.org/10.1080/10410236.2017.1331184.

Jiang, L. C., Sun, M., Chu, T. H., & Chia, S. C. (2022). Inoculation works and health advocacy backfires: Building resistance to COVID-19 vaccine misinformation in a low political trust context. *Frontiers in Psychology, 13*, 976091. https://doi.org/10.3389/fpsyg.2022.976091.

Johnson, B. T., & Eagly, A. H. (1989). Effects of involvement on persuasion: A meta-analysis. *Psychological Bulletin, 106*(2), 290–314. https://doi.org/10.1037/0033-2909.106.2.290.

Kahneman, D. (2013). *Thinking, fast and slow.* Farrar, Straus and Giroux.

Kemp, P. L., Loaiza, V. M., & Wahlheim, C. N. (2022). Fake news reminders and veracity labels differentially benefit memory and belief accuracy for news headlines. *Scientific Reports, 12*(1), 1–13. https://doi.org/10.1038/s41598-022-25649-6.

Knobloch-Westerwick, S., & Meng, J. (2011). Reinforcement of the political self through selective exposure to political messages. *Journal of Communication, 61*(2), 349–368. https://doi.org/10.1111/j.1460-2466.2011.01543.x.

Knobloch-Westerwick, S., Westerwick, A., & Johnson, B. (2015). Selective exposure in the communication technology context. In S. S. Sundar (Ed.), *Handbook of the psychology of communication technology* (pp. 407–427). Wiley-Blackwell.

Kouzy, R., Abi Jaoude, J., Kraitem, A. et al. (2020). Coronavirus goes viral: Quantifying the COVID-19 misinformation epidemic on Twitter. *Cureus, 12* (3), **e7255.** https://doi.org/10.7759/cureus.7255.

Krause, N. M., Freiling, I., Beets, B., & Brossard, D. (2020). Fact-checking as risk communication: The multi-layered risk of misinformation in times of COVID-19. *Journal of Risk Research, 23*(7–8), 1052–1059. https://doi.org/10.1080/13669877.2020.1756385.

Krause, N. M., Freiling, I., & Scheufele, D. A. (2022). The "infodemic" infodemic: Toward a more nuanced understanding of truth-claims and the need for (not) combatting misinformation. *The ANNALS of the American*

Academy of Political and Social Science, *700*(1), 112–123. https://doi.org/10.1177/00027162221086263.

Kuklinski, J. H., Quirk, P. J., Jerit, J., Schwieder, D., & Rich, R. F. (2000). Misinformation and the currency of democratic citizenship. *The Journal of Politics*, *62*(3), 790–816. https://doi.org/10.1111/0022-3816.00033.

Kunda, Z. (1990). The case for motivated reasoning. *Psychological Bulletin*, *108*(3), 480–498. https://doi.org/10.1037/0033-2909.108.3.480.

Lazer, D. M., Baum, M. A., Benkler, Y. et al. (2018). The science of fake news. *Science*, *359*(6380), 1094–1096. https://doi.org/10.1126/science.aao2998.

Lees, J., Banas, J. A., Linvill, D., Meirick, P. C., & Warren, P. (2023). The Spot the Troll Quiz game increases accuracy in discerning between real and in authentic social media accounts. *PNAS Nexus*, *2*, 1–11. https://doi.org/10.1093/pnasnexus/pgad094.

Lewandowsky, S., Ecker, U. K., & Cook, J. (2017). Beyond misinformation: Understanding and coping with the "post-truth" era. *Journal of Applied Research in Memory and Cognition*, *6*(4), 353–369. https://doi.org/10.1016/j.jarmac.2017.07.008.

Lewandowsky, S., & Van Der Linden, S. (2021). Countering misinformation and fake news through inoculation and prebunking. *European Review of Social Psychology*, *32*(2), 348–384. https://doi.org/10.1080/10463283.2021.1876983.

Lin, W. W. K. (2022). Enhancing inoculation in the spiral of silence to promote resistance to attacks: Examining public opinion on Taiwan-PRC relations. *Asian Journal for Public Opinion Research*, *10*(3), 149–177. https://doi.org/10.15206/ajpor.2022.10.3.149.

Lin, W.-K., & Pfau, M. (2007). Can inoculation work against the spiral of silence? A study of public opinion on the future of Taiwan. *International Journal of Public Opinion Research*, *19*(2), 155–172. https://doi.org/10.1093/ijpor/edl030.

Loomba, S., de Figueiredo, A., Piatek, S. J., de Graaf, K., & Larson, H. J. (2021). Measuring the impact of COVID-19 vaccine misinformation on vaccination intent in the UK and USA. *Nature Human Behaviour*, *5*(5), 337–348. https://doi.org/10.1038/s41562-021-01056-1.

Lu, C., Hu, B., Li, Q., Bi, C., & Ju, X.-D. (2023). Psychological inoculation for credibility assessment, sharing intention, and discernment of misinformation: Systematic review and meta-analysis. *Journal of Medical Internet Research*, *25*(1), e49255. https://doi.org/10.2196/49255.

Lumsdaine, A. A., & Janis, I. L. (1953). Resistance to "counterpropaganda" produced by one-sided and two-sided "propaganda" presentations. *Public Opinion Quarterly*, *17*(3), 311–318. https://doi.org/10.1086/266464.

Maertens, R., Anseel, F., & van der Linden, S. (2020). Combatting climate change misinformation: Evidence for longevity of inoculation and consensus messaging effects. *Journal of Environmental Psychology, 70,* 101455. https://doi.org/10.1016/j.jenvp.2020.101455.

Maertens, R., Roozenbeek, J., Basol, M., & van der Linden, S. (2021). Long-term effectiveness of inoculation against misinformation: Three longitudinal experiments. *Journal of Experimental Psychology: Applied, 27*(1), 1–16. https://doi.org/10.1037/xap0000315.supp.

Martel, C., Mosleh, M., & Rand, D. G. (2021). You're definitely wrong, maybe: Correction style has minimal effect on corrections of misinformation online. *Media and Communication, 9*(1), 120–133. https://doi.org/10.17645/mac.v9i1.3519.

Mason, A. M., Compton, J., Tice, E. et al. (2024). Analyzing the prophylactic and therapeutic role of inoculation to facilitate resistance to conspiracy theory beliefs. *Communication Reports, 37*(1), 13–27. https://doi.org/10.1080/08934215.2023.2256803.

McGuire, W. J. (1961). The effectiveness of supportive and refutational defenses in immunizing and restoring beliefs against persuasion. *Sociometry, 24*(2), 184–197. https://doi.org/10.2307/2786067.

McGuire, W. J. (1962). Persistence of the resistance to persuasion induced by various types of prior belief defenses. *The Journal of Abnormal and Social Psychology, 64*(4), 241–248. https://doi.org/10.1037/h0044167.

McGuire, W. J. (1964). Inducing resistance to persuasion: Some contemporary approaches. *Advances in Experimental Social Psychology, 1,* 191–229. https://doi.org/10.1016/S00652601(08)60052-0.

McGuire, W. J., & Papageorgis, D. (1961). The relative efficacy of various types of prior belief-defense in producing immunity against persuasion. *The Journal of Abnormal and Social Psychology, 62*(2), 327–337. https://doi.org/10.1037/h0042026.

McGuire, W. J., & Papageorgis, D. (1962). Effectiveness of forewarning in developing resistance to persuasion. *Public Opinion Quarterly, 26*(1), 24–34. https://doi.org/10.1086/267068.

McQuade, B. (2024). *Attack from within: How disinformation is sabotaging America.* Seven Stories Press.

Mikolon, S., Quaiser, B., & Wieseke, J. (2015). Don't try harder: Using customer inoculation to build resistance against service failures. *Journal of the Academy of Marketing Science, 43,* 512–527. https://doi.org/10.1007/s11747-014-0398-1.

Miller, C. H., Ivanov, B., Sims, J. et al. (2013). Boosting the potency of resistance: Combining the motivational forces of inoculation and psychological

reactance. *Human Communication Research, 39*(1), 127–155. https://doi.org/
10.1111/j.1468-2958.2012.01438.x.

Motta, M., Callaghan, T., & Sylvester, S. (2018). Knowing less but presuming
more: Dunning-Kruger effects and the endorsement of anti-vaccine policy
attitudes. *Social Science & Medicine, 211*(211), 274–281. https://doi.org/
10.1016/j.socscimed.2018.06.032.

Nabi, R. L. (2003). "Feeling" resistance: Exploring the role of emotionally
evocative visuals in inducing inoculation. *Media Psychology, 5*(2), 199–223.
https://doi.org/10.1207/S1532785XMEP0502_4.

Nagel, J. (2010). Knowledge ascriptions and the psychological consequences of
thinking about error. *The Philosophical Quarterly, 60*(239), 286–306. https://
doi.org/10.1111/j.1467-9213.2009.624.x.

Nan, X., Thier, K., & Wang, Y. (2023). Health misinformation: what it is, why
people believe it, how to counter it. *Annals of the International Communication
Association, 47*(4), 381–410. https://doi.org/10.1080/23808985.2023.2225489.

Nan, X., Wang, Y., & Thier, K. (2022). Why do people believe health misinformation and who are at risk? A systematic review of individual differences in
susceptibility to health misinformation. *Social Science & Medicine, 314*,
115398. https://doi.org/10.1016/j.socscimed.2022.115398.

National Cancer Institute (2004). *Making health communication programs
work.*

Newman, T. P., Nisbet, E. C., & Nisbet, M. C. (2018). Climate change, cultural
cognition, and media effects: Worldviews drive news selectivity, biased
processing, and polarized attitudes. *Public Understanding of Science, 27*
(8), 985–1002. https://doi.org/10.1177/0963662518801170.

Novilla, M. L. B., Goates, M. C., Redelfs, A. H. et al. (2023). Why parents say
no to having their children vaccinated against Measles: A systematic review
of the social determinants of parental perceptions on MMR vaccine
hesitancy. *Vaccines, 11*(5), 926. https://doi.org/10.3390/vaccines11050926.

Nyhan, B., & Reifler, J. (2010). When corrections fail: The persistence of
political misperceptions. *Political Behavior, 32*(2), 303–330. https://doi
.org/10.1007/s11109-010-9112-2.

Osgood, C. E., & Tannenbaum, P. H. (1955). The principle of congruity in the
prediction of attitude change. *Psychological Review, 62*(1), 42–55. https://
doi.org/10.1037/h0048153.

Pandey, A., & Galvani, A. P. (2023). Exacerbation of measles mortality by
vaccine hesitancy worldwide. *The Lancet Global Health, 11*(4), e478–e479.
https://doi.org/10.1016/S2214-109X(23)00063-3.

Papageorgis, D., & McGuire, W. J. (1961). The generality of immunity to
persuasion produced by pre-exposure to weakened counterarguments. *The*

Journal of Abnormal and Social Psychology, 62(3), 475–481. https://doi.org/10.1037/h0048430.

Parker, K. A., Ivanov, B., & Compton, J. (2012). Inoculation's efficacy with young adults' risky behaviors: Can inoculation confer cross-protection over related but untreated issues? *Health Communication, 27*(3), 223–233. https://doi.org/10.1080/10410236.2011.575541.

Parker, K. A., Ivanov, B., Matig, J., Dillingham, L. L., & Peritore, N. (2022). Inoculation booster messages: Frequency, content, and timing. *The Journal of Communication and Media Studies, 7*(1), 1–19. https://doi.org/10.18848/2470-9247/CGP/v07i01/1-19.

Petrocelli, J. V., Tormala, Z. L., & Rucker, D. D. (2007). Unpacking attitude certainty: Attitude clarity and attitude correctness. *Journal of Personality and Social Psychology, 92*(1), 30–41. https://doi.org/10.1037/0022-3514.92.1.30.

Petty, R. E., & Cacioppo, J. T. (1979). Issue involvement can increase or decrease persuasion by enhancing message-relevant cognitive responses. *Journal of Personality and Social Psychology, 37*(10), 1915–1926. https://doi.org/10.1037/0022-3514.37.10.1915.

Petty, R. E., & Cacioppo, J. T. (1986). The elaboration likelihood model of persuasion. In Berkowitz (Ed.), *Advances in experimental social psychology* (Vol. 19, pp. 123–205). Academic Press.

Pfau, M. (1997). The inoculation model of resistance to influence. In G. A. Barnett & F. J. Boster (Eds.), *Progress in communication sciences: Advances in persuasion* (Vol. 13, pp. 133–171). Ablex.

Pfau, M., & Bockern, S. V. (1994). The persistence of inoculation in conferring resistance to smoking initiation among adolescents: The second year. *Human Communication Research, 20*(3), 413–430. https://doi.org/10.1111/j.1468-2958.1994.tb00329.x.

Pfau, M., Bockern, S. V., & Kang, J. G. (1992). Use of inoculation to promote resistance to smoking initiation among adolescents. *Communication Monographs, 59*(3), 213–230. https://doi.org/10.1080/03637759209376266.

Pfau, M., & Burgoon, M. (1988). Inoculation in political campaign communication. *Human Communication Research, 15*(1), 91–111. https://doi.org/10.1111/j.1468-2958.1988.tb00172.x.

Pfau, M., Compton, J., Parker, K. A. et al. (2004). The traditional explanation for resistance versus attitude accessibility: Do they trigger distinct or overlapping processes of resistance? *Human Communication Research, 30*(3), 329–360. https://doi.org/10.1093/hcr/30.3.329.

Pfau, M., & Kenski, H. C. (1990). *Attack politics: Strategy and defense*. Praeger.

Pfau, M., Park, D., Holbert, R. L., & Cho, J. (2001). The effects of party- and PAC-sponsored issue advertising and the potential of inoculation to combat its impact on the democratic process. *American Behavioral Scientist, 44*(12), 2379–2397. https://doi.org/10.1177/00027640121958384.

Pfau, M., Tusing, K. J., Koerner, A. F. et al. (1997). Enriching the inoculation construct: The role of critical components in the process of resistance. *Human Communication Research, 24*(2), 187–215. https://doi.org/10.1111/j.1468-2958.1997.tb00413.x.

Pluviano, S., Watt, C., & Della Sala, S. (2017). Misinformation lingers in memory: Failure of three pro-vaccination strategies. *PloS One, 12*(7), e0181640. https://doi.org/10.1371/journal.pone.0181640.

Preston, S. D., & de Waal, F. B. M. (2002). Empathy: Its ultimate and proximate bases. *Behavioral and Brain Sciences, 25*(1), 1–20. https://doi.org/10.1017/s0140525x02000018.

Putman, A. L., Sungkhasettee, V. W., & Roediger, III, H. L. (2017). When misinformation improves memory: The effects of recollecting change. *Psychological Science, 28*(1), 36–46. https://doi.org/10.1177/0956797616672268.

Reich, J. A. (2016). *Calling the shots: Why parents reject vaccines*. New York University Press.

Rich, P. R., & Zaragoza, M. S. (2020). Correcting misinformation in news stories: An investigation of correction timing and correction durability. *Journal of Applied Research in Memory and Cognition, 9*(3), 310–322. https://doi.org/10.1037/h0101850.

Richards, A. S., & Banas, J. A. (2015). Inoculating against reactance to persuasive health messages. *Health Communication, 30*(5), 451–460. https://doi.org/10.1080/10410236.2013.867005.

Richards, A. S., & Banas, J. A. (2018). The opposing mediational effects of apprehensive threat and motivational threat when inoculating against reactance to health promotion. *The Southern Communication Journal, 83*(4), 245–255. https://doi.org/10.1080/1041794X.2018.1498909.

Richards, A. S., Banas, J. A., & Magid, Y. (2017). More on inoculating against reactance to persuasive health messages: The paradox of threat. *Health Communication, 32*(7), 890–902. https://doi.org/10.1080/10410236.2016.1196410.

Richards, A. S., Bessarabova, E., Banas, J. A., & Larsen, M. (2021). Freedom-prompting reactance mitigation strategies function differently across levels of trait reactance. *Communication Quarterly, 69*(3), 238–258. https://doi.org/10.1080/01463373.2021.1920443.

Rogers, R. W., & Thistlethwaite, D. L. (1969). An analysis of active and passive defenses in inducing resistance to persuasion. *Journal of Personality and Social Psychology, 11*(4), 301–308. https://doi.org/10.1037/h0027354.

Roozenbeek, J., & van der Linden, S. (2019a). The fake news game: Actively inoculating against the risk of misinformation. *Journal of Risk Research, 22* (5), 570–580. https://doi.org/10.1080/13669877.2018.1443491.

Roozenbeek, J., & van der Linden, S. (2019b). Fake news game confers psychological resistance against online misinformation. *Palgrave Communications, 5* (1), 1–10. https://doi.org/10.1057/s41599-019-0279-9.

Roozenbeek, J., & van der Linden, S. (2020). Breaking Harmony Square: A game that "inoculates" against political misinformation. *Harvard Kennedy School Misinformation Review, 1*(8). https://doi.org/10.37016/mr-2020-47.

Roozenbeek, J., Van Der Linden, S., Goldberg, B., Rathje, S., & Lewandowsky, S. (2022). Psychological inoculation improves resilience against misinformation on social media. *Science Advances, 8*(34), eabo6254. https://doi.org/10.1126/sciadv.abo6254.

Roozenbeek, J., van der Linden, S., & Nygren, T. (2020). Prebunking interventions based on the psychological theory of "inoculation" can reduce susceptibility to misinformation across cultures. *Harvard Kennedy School Misinformation Review.* https://doi.org/10.37016//mr-2020-008.

Roozenbeek, J., Maertens, R., McClanahan, W., & van der Linden, S. (2021). Disentangling item and testing effects in inoculation research on online misinformation: Solomon revisited. *Educational and Psychological Measurement, 81*(2), 340–362. https://doi.org/10.1177/0013164420940378.

Sangalang, A., Ophir, Y., & Cappella, J. N. (2019). The potential for narrative correctives to combat misinformation. *Journal of Communication, 69*(3), 298–319. https://doi.org/10.1093/joc/jqz014.

Seifert, C. M. (2002). The continued influence of misinformation in memory: What makes a correction effective? *Psychology of Learning and Motivation, 41*, 265–292. https://doi.org/10.1016/S0079-7421(02)80009-3.

Seifert, C. M. (2014). The continued influence effect: The persistence of misinformation in memory and reasoning following correction. In D. N. Rapp & J. L. G. Braasch (Eds.), *Processing inaccurate information: Theoretical and applied perspectives from cognitive science and the educational science* (pp. 39–71). MIT Press.

Sharot, T., & Sunstein, C. R. (2020). How people decide what they want to know. *Nature Human Behaviour, 4*(1), 14–19. https://doi.org/10.1038/s41562-019-0793-1.

Shen, L. (2010). On a scale of state empathy during message processing. *Western Journal of Communication, 74*(5), 504–524. https://doi.org/10.1080/10570314.2010.512278.

Shen, L., & Zhou, Y. (2021). Epistemic egocentrism and processing of vaccine misinformation (vis-à-vis scientific evidence): The case of vaccine-autism link. *Health Communication, 36*(11), 1405–1416. https://doi.org/10.1080/10410236.2020.1761074.

Sherif, M., & Hovland, C. I. (1961). *Social judgment: Assimilation and contrast effects in communication and attitude change.* Yale University Press.

Sherif, C. W., Kelly, M., Rodgers Jr, H. L., Sarup, G., & Tittler, B. I. (1973). Personal involvement, social judgment, and action. *Journal of Personality and Social Psychology, 27*(3), 311–328. https://doi.org/10.1037/h0034948.

Sherif, C. W., Sherif, M., & Nebergall, R. E. (1965). *Attitude and attitude change: The social judgment-involvement approach.* Saunders Philadelphia.

Sherman, D. K., & Cohen, G. L. (2002). Accepting threatening information: Self-affirmation and the reduction of defensive biases. *Current Directions in Psychological Science, 11*(4), 119–123. https://doi.org/10.1111/1467-8721.00182.

Southwell, B. G., Otero Machuca, J., Cherry, S. T., Burnside, M., & Barrett, N. J. (2023). Health misinformation exposure and health disparities: Observations and opportunities. *Annual Review of Public Health, 44*(1), 113–130. https://doi.org/10.1146/annurev-publhealth-071321-031118.

Southwell, B. G., & Yzer, M. C. (2007). The roles of interpersonal communication in mass media campaigns. *Annals of the International Communication Association, 31*(1), 420–462. https://doi.org/10.1080/23808985.2007.11679072.

Spampatti, T., Hahnel, U. J. J., Trutnevyte, E., & Brosch, T. (2024). Psychological inoculation strategies to fight climate disinformation across 12 countries. *Nature Human Behavior, 8*(2), 380–398. https://doi.org/10.1038/s41562-023-01736-0.

Staender, A., Humprecht, E., Esser, F., Morosoli, S., & van Aelst, P. (2022). Is sensationalist disinformation more effective? Three facilitating factors at the national, individual, and situational level. *Digital Journalism, 10*(6), 976–996. https://doi.org/10.1080/21670811.2021.1966315.

Stop Funding Heat (2021). *In denial: Facebook's growing friendship with climate misinformation.* https://stopfundingheat.info/wp-content/uploads/2021/11/in-denial-v2.pdf

Szabo, E. A., & Pfau, M. (2001, November). *Reactance as a response to anti-smoking messages.* Paper presented at the annual meeting of the National Communication Association, Atlanta, GA.

Täuber, S., van Zomeren, M., & Kutlaca, M. (2015). Should the moral core of climate issues be emphasized or downplayed in public discourse? Three ways to successfully manage the double-edged sword of moral communication. *Climatic Change, 130*(3), 453–464. https://doi.org/10.1007/s10584-014-1200-6.

Thorson, E. (2016). Belief echoes: The persistent effects of corrected misinformation. *Political Communication, 33*(3), 460–480. https://doi.org/10.1080/10584609.2015.1102187.

Treen, K. M. d'I., Williams, H. T. P., & O'Neill, S. J. (2020). Online misinformation about climate change. *WIREs Climate Change, 11*(5), e665. https://doi.org/10.1002/wcc.665.

van der Linden, S. (2022). Misinformation: Susceptibility, spread, and interventions to immunize the public. *Nature Medicine, 28*(3), 460–467. https://doi.org/10.1038/s41591-022-01713-6.

van der Linden, S., Leiserowitz, A., Rosenthal, S., & Maibach, E. (2017). Inoculating the public against misinformation about climate change. *Global Challenges, 1*(2), 1600008. https://doi.org/10.1002/gch2.201600008.

van der Linden, S., Maibach, E., Cook, J., Leiserowitz, A., & Lewandowsky, S. (2017). Inoculating against misinformation. *Science, 358*(6367), 1141–1142. https://doi.org/10.1126/science.aar4533.

van der Meer, T. G. L. A., & Jin, Y. (2019). Seeking formula for misinformation treatment in public health crises: The effects of corrective information type and source. *Health Communication, 35*(5), 560–575. https://doi.org/10.1080/10410236.2019.1573295.

van Oostendorp, H. (1996). Updating situation models derived from newspaper articles. *Medienpsychologie, 8*, 21–33.

van Strien, J. L. H., Kammerer, Y., Brand-Gruwel, S., & Boshuizen, H. P. A. (2016). How attitude strength biases information processing and evaluation on the web. *Computers in Human Behavior, 60*, 245–252. https://doi.org/10.1016/j.chb.2016.02.057.

Vosoughi, S., Roy, D., & Aral, S. (2018). The spread of true and false news online. *Science, 359*(6380), 1146–1151. https://doi.org/10.1126/science.aap9559.

Vraga, E. K., & Bode, L. (2020). Defining misinformation and understanding its bounded nature: Using expertise and evidence for describing misinformation. *Political Communication, 37*(1), 136–144. https://doi.org/10.1080/10584609.2020.1716500.

Vraga, E. K., Kim, S. C., & Cook, J. (2019). Testing logic-based and humor-based corrections for science, health, and political misinformation on social media. *Journal of Broadcasting & Electronic Media, 63*(3), 393–414. https://doi.org/10.1080/08838151.2019.1653102.

Vraga, E. K., Kim, S. C., Cook, J., & Bode, L. (2020). Testing the effectiveness of correction placement and type on Instagram. *The International Journal of Press/Politics, 25*(4), 632–652. https://doi.org/10.1177/1940161220919082.

Walter, N., & Murphy, S. T. (2018). How to unring the bell: A meta-analytic approach to correction of misinformation. *Communication Monographs, 85*(3), 423–441. https://doi.org/10.1080/03637751.2018.1467564.

Walter, N., & Tukachinsky, R. (2020). A meta-analytic examination of the continued influence of misinformation in the face of correction: How powerful is it, why does it happen, and how to stop it? *Communication Research, 47* (2), 155–177. https://doi.org/10.1177/0093650219854600.

Wang, Y., Thier, K., & Nan, X. (2022). Defining health misinformation. In A. Keselman, C. A. Smith, & A. Wilson (Eds.), *Combating online health misinformation: A professional's guide to helping the public* (pp. 3–16). Palgrave Macmillan.

Wardle, C. (2017). *Fake news: It's complicated*. First draft.

Williams, M. N., & Bond, C. M. C. (2020). A preregistered replication of "Inoculating the public against misinformation about climate change." *Journal of Environmental Psychology, 70*, 101456. https://doi.org/10.1016/j.jenvp.2020.101456.

Wischnewski, M., & Krämer, N. (2020, July). *I reason who I am? Identity salience manipulation to reduce motivated reasoning in news consumption.* International Conference on Social Media and Society.

Wood, M. L. M. (2007). Rethinking the inoculation analogy: Effects on subjects with differing preexisting attitudes. *Human Communication Research, 33*(3), 357–378. https://doi.org/10.1111/j.1468-2958.2007.00303.x.

Wyer, R. S. (1974). *Cognitive organization and change: An information processing approach*. Taylor & Francis.

Xu, S., Coman, I. A., Yamamoto, M., & Najera, C. J. (2023). Exposure effects or confirmation bias? Examining reciprocal dynamics of misinformation, misperceptions, and attitudes toward COVID-19 vaccines. *Health Communication, 38* (10), 2210–2220. https://doi.org/10.1080/10410236.2022.2059802.

Zerback, T., Töpfl, F., & Knöpfle, M. (2021). The disconcerting potential of online disinformation: Persuasive effects of astroturfing comments and three strategies for inoculation against them. *New Media & Society, 23*(5), 1080–1098. https://doi.org/10.1177/1461444820908530.

Zhao, X., & Fink, E. L. (2021). Proattitudinal versus counterattitudinal messages: Message discrepancy, reactance, and the boomerang effect. *Communication Monographs, 88*(3), 286–305. https://doi.org/10.1080/03637751.2020.1813317.

Zhou, Y., & Shen, L. (2022). Confirmation bias and the persistence of misinformation on climate change. *Communication Research, 49*(4), 500–523. https://doi.org/10.1177/00936502211028049.

Zia, A., & Todd, A. M. (2010). Evaluating the effects of ideology on public understanding of climate change science: How to improve communication across ideological divides? *Public Understanding of Science, 19*(6), 743–761. https://doi.org/10.1177/0963662509357871.

Cambridge Elements ☰

Health Communication

Louise Cummings
The Hong Kong Polytechnic University

Louise Cummings is Professor in the Department of English and Communication at The Hong Kong Polytechnic University. She conducts research in health communication and clinical linguistics and is the author and editor of over 20 books in these areas. Prof. Cummings is a member of the Royal College of Speech and Language Therapists and the Health & Care Professions Council in the UK.

About the Series

This series brings together a wide range of disciplines that converge on the study of communication in health settings. Each element examines a key topic in health communication and is carefully crafted by experts in their respective disciplines. The series is relevant to students, researchers, and practitioners in humanities, medical and health professions, and social scientific disciplines.

Cambridge Elements⁼

Health Communication

Elements in the Series

Worse Than Ignorance: The Challenge of Health Misinformation
Peter J. Schulz and Kent Nakamoto

Protecting the Public's Health during Novel Infectious Disease Outbreaks
Louise Cummings

Persistence of Misinformation: Biased Cognitive Processing and Polarization
Yanmengqian Zhou and Lijiang Shen

A full series listing is available at: www.cambridge.org/EIHC